Chinese Calligraphy Teach Yourself Series

A Self-Study Course in Running Script

Compiled and written by Huang Quanxin

SINOLINGUA

BEIJING

First Edition   1998

ISBN 7-80052-456-6

Copyright 1998 by Sinolingua

Published by Sinolingua

24 Baiwanzhuang Road, Beijing 100037, China

Printed by Chunlei Printing House

Distributed by China International

Book Trading Corporation

35 Chegongzhuang Xilu, P.O. Box 399

Beijing 100044, China

Printed in the People's Republic of China

Foreword

Chinese calligraphy, the core of the Oriental arts, reflects the temperament of the Chinese nation. The black and white, dots and lines are an expression of the spirits and images of Nature, reflecting a calligrapher's feelings and knowledge. Calligraphy's profound artistic essence lies in the combination of feeling and rationale, form and spirit, rich structure and vivid rhythm – a perfect balance between the form and the ideological content expressed in a character. Though devoid of color, calligraphy is variously colored as painting; and without sound, it contains melodies just like music.

Chinese calligraphy has a long history, ranging from the keeping of records by tying knots before Cang Jie invented writing, to the characters on earthenware discovered at Dawenkou and inscriptions on bones or tortoise shells of the Shang Dynasty (c. 16th-11th century BC). Like a long running river, Chinese calligraphy has evolved during thousands of years, characterized by simplicity and unsophistication in the Shang and Zhou dynasties (c. 16th century-221 BC), splendor in the Qin and Han dynasties (221 BC-AD 220), graceful bearing in the Wei and Jin dynasties (220-420), magnificence in the Sui and Tang dynasties (581-907), radiating vigor in the Song and Yuan dynasties (960-1368), prosperity in the Ming and Qing dynasties (1368-1911) and grandeur in the current era.

Chinese characters fall into the following styles: regular, running, grass, official and seal scripts. Seal scripts may be divided into large and small characters; official scripts, into Qin and Han styles; grass characters, into *Zhang* (cursive official), *Jin* (modern) and *Kuang* (wild) scripts; and regular characters, into Wei and Tang scripts. Chinese calligraphy not only reflects the character of individual calligrapher, but also presents the styles and flavors of different regions and eras.

China has always regarded calligraphy as the quintessence of Chinese culture and a national treasure as well. Calligraphy is a required course at school and every educated person must study calligraphy.

The art of Chinese calligraphy is unprecedentedly prosperous now. Various kinds of calligraphy model books have been published; however, it is hard to find one which can scientifically instruct people in learning calligraphy. An old saying goes: ``If one owns the best book, one may obtain medium-level knowledge; and if one has a medium-level book, one may only absorb low-level knowledge." Anyone who wishes to have a good command of Chinese calligraphy must have a good teacher and a good book. At the present time when it is hard to find a good teacher, good teaching materials are even more important.

To meet the demands of the people who are interested in Chinese calligraphy, Professor Huang Quanxin has compiled the *Chinese Calligraphy Teach-Yourself Series* in six books: *A Self-Study Course in Regular Script*, *A Self-Study Course in Wei Stone Inscriptions*, *A Self-Study Course in Running Script*, *A Self-Study Course in Grass Script*, *A Self-Study Course in Official Script*, and *A Self-Study Course in Seal Script*. Each book consists of the following chapters: A Brief Introduction, Techniques, Strokes, Radicals, Structure, The Art of Composition, Creation, Copying, and Appreciation, which should help beginners learn the rudiments, and other learners improve their calligraphy techniques.

With standard model characters, systematic theories for self-study, illustration and texts, the *Chinese Calligraphy Teach-Yourself Series* is well formatted, informative and interesting. Student may appreciate Chinese calligraphy while practicing the models in the books to improve their accomplishments and techniques. We sincerely wish they are of help with the study of Chinese calligraphy.

Editor
October 1994

About the Author

Huang Quanxin is a senior teacher of fine arts in the Middle School Attached to Beijing Normal University and a member of the Chinese Calligraphers' Association. In his childhood, he took up the study of calligraphy and paintings, and read a large number of poems. His father was a student of Kang Youwei (a famous reformist in the late Qing Dynasty). For many years, he has lived in Liulichang (an ancient cultural street in Beijing), taken many famous calligraphers, scholars and experts as his teachers, and immersed himself untiringly among calligraphy and painting. When he was a middle-school student, he won first place in a calligraphy contest. Later many more works won awards at important calligraphy competitions and have been exhibited at home and abroad. In addition, he has inscribed the titles of many newspapers and magazines. He is named as an eminent person of the contemporary era by the Calligraphy Association of Wang Xizhi's hometown, included in the book *Famous Calligraphers in Beijing* by the Beijing Calligraphers' Association, as well as in *A Dictionary of Chinese Artists of the Present Age* and *Who's Who in the World*.

Huang Quanxin is also a member of the Chinese Society for Fine Arts Education and a standing council member of the district society. In his youth, he compiled teaching materials for the fine arts, painted color picture-story books, and created hanging paintings, which were named by the State Education Commission as excellent works. He visited Taiwan as a member of the artists delegation from mainland China and held a one-man calligraphy show in Japan. Many of his calligraphy works and paintings have been sent by the government officials to foreign guests as gifts, enjoying a high reputation both at home and abroad. Hence he is included in the book *Famous Chinese Painters*.

Huang Quanxin has served as teacher for thirty years, with students from all over the country and some in foreign countries. Quite a number of his students came out top at many domestic and international calligraphy and paintings competitions.

Huang Quanxin founded the first parents' school in Beijing and has served as head of the National Excellent Parents' School for many years. He is a consultant of Beijing primary and middle-school education, a former host of an education program of Beijing Broadcasting Station, one of the compilers of the teaching materials and courses of the Beijing Parents' School, a member of the Beijing Research Association of Family Education and a council member of the district research association. He is also interested in various aspects of Chinese traditional culture and arts, and serves as a council member of the Association for Developing Beijing and Kunqu Operas.

Huang Quanxin has devoted his spare time to the study of calligraphy, paintings and other Chinese traditional culture and arts as well as to the education of arts. Up to now more than thirty of his books have been published, including *Grand View of China's Auspiciousness Series*, *The Series of Authentic Characters of Fu (fortune)*, *Lu (emoluments)*, *Shou (longevity)* and *Xi (happiness) by Famous Calligraphers of Past Dynasties*, *Modern Inscriptions*, *A Copybook of Ancient Chinese Poems*, *An Intense Course for Practical Fountain Pen Handwriting*, and *Elementary Handwriting for Young People*. In addition he has been a designer for many books. Huang Quanxin, who enjoys a high reputation in China and abroad, is included in the *Directory of Eminent Literary Personnel of China* by the Research Institute of Literature of the China Academy of Social Sciences.

Contents

Chapter I　Running Script

1. Origin of Running Script

Running script originated at the end of the Han Dynasty (206 BC-220) and was said to be created by Liu Desheng. It was not until the Jin Dynasty (265-420) that the script was perfected by Wang Xizhi. Running script is as vivid and simple as grass script, and is dignified and easy to read and write like regular script. Chinese forefathers spoke highly of running script: "Straight and graceful running characters, controlled by a calligrapher's feelings and spirit, can be written as one wishes, like the running wind, scattered rain, and beautiful flowers in full bloom. Hence running script is the most distinguished of the various Chinese scripts."

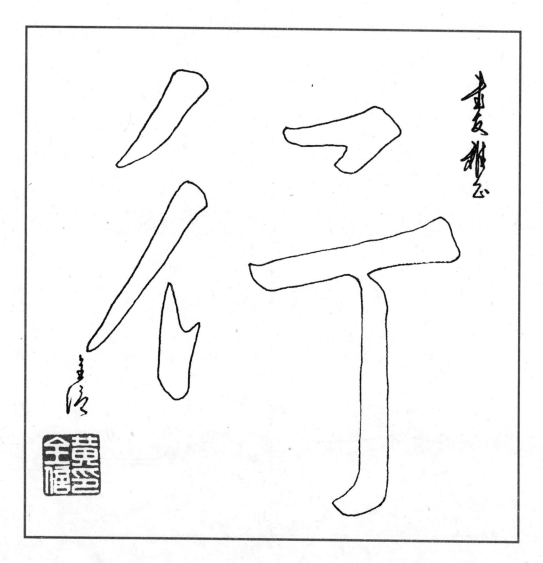

2. Powerful and Rapid Movement of the Brush

"If regular characters may be likened to a person standing straight and still, running characters are like a person strolling along in a leisurely manner, and grass characters are like one running rapidly." In running script, "running" means vivid, easy and smooth, with strokes like flowing clouds and running water. Running characters, which take *qi* (vital energy) as the mainstay and strength as supplements, can be written faster than regular characters in light and clear-cut rhythm, showing the basic form of regular script and the flowing style of grass script. Hence running script has been loved by people for over a thousand years. Running script has not only high artistic value, but also the most extensively practical value.

3. Naturally Broken and Connected Strokes

In running script, round cornering strokes replace square cornering strokes of regular script, dots replace strokes, and simple strokes, complex ones. It is easy to write and read running characters. Echoes among strokes in running script are more obvious than in regular script. More often than not, there are connected strokes, thin additional linking lines (very thin lines that link strokes) and additional small hooks (tiny hooks appearing in the movement of the brush that link strokes) in running characters. Running script is known for its naturally broken and connected strokes. Regular script has clear-cut dots and strokes, showing stable movement of the brush. However the strokes in running script are flowing, displaying vivid movement of the brush.

4. Various Beautiful Shapes

Running script is a script between regular and grass scripts. In a running script works, one may sometimes find regular characters, and sometimes grass characters, a style particular to running script. Those written like regular characters are known as "running regular script"; and those more like grass characters are named as "running grass script."

Running characters, not like square and neatly written regular script, are now large and now small, now round and now square, now moving and now still, now rash and now smooth, showing various beautiful shapes.

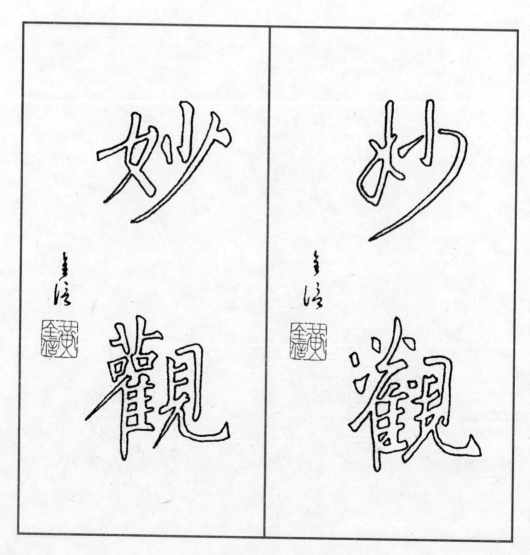

Chapter II   Techniques of Writing

1. Sitting Position

The head: One should hold the head straight, inclined slightly forward, look at the copybook and keep the mind peaceful.

The body: One should sit straight, keep the shoulders level and the waist stiff, and should not touch the table edge with the chest.

The arms: One should relax one's arms, the left hand resting on the paper and the right hand holding the brush.

The feet: One should rest one's feet parallel on the floor, the legs relaxed and the body stable.

2. Standing Position

When writing large Chinese characters, one should stand, with the elbow suspended.

Hold the head straight, incline the body slightly forward, look at the copybook and keep the mind peaceful.

Hold the brush with the right hand, place the left hand on the table, and suspend the elbow while writing characters to freely express one's feeling.

Place the right foot slightly forward and the left foot slightly back, and rest the soles flat on the floor with the center of gravity on the right foot.

Write characters with the strength from the waist and the roots of the foot to make every stroke penetrate the paper.

3. Holding the Brush

One should hold the brush with fingers, keep the palm hollow and the brush shaft straight.

Pushing down: The thumb pushes the brush from inside to outside.

Pressing: The index finger presses the brush from outside to inside.

Hooking: The middle finger pulls the brush from outside on the left to inside on the right.

Squaring: The ring finger pushes the brush from inside on the right to outside on the left.

Supporting: The little finger gives auxiliary strength to the ring finger.

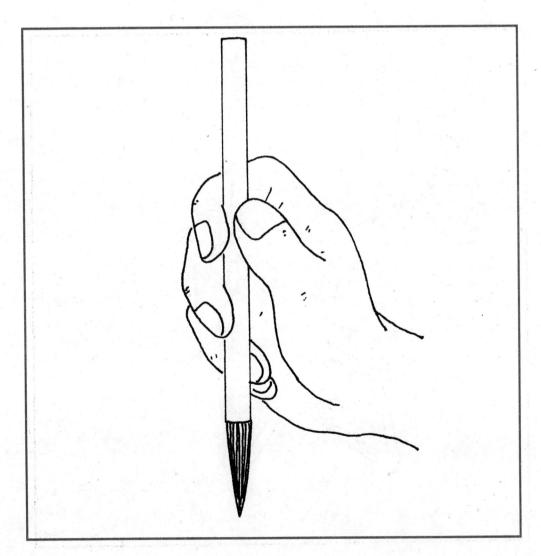

4. Movement of the Brush

One moves the brush with the wrist. If the middle point of the brush is used in the movement of the brush, all strength will be concentrated on the writing brush and strokes will be full of spirit. The contrary-point method is used to start a stroke; the middle-point method, to move the brush on; and the hidden-point method, to close a stroke.

In writing running script, one should basically follow the rules of regular script. But running characters, written at a faster speed, have more exposed points, more ups and downs and a strong sense of rhythm. One must pay particular attention to handling the connections between dots and strokes which should be written powerfully, and the thin linking lines between them which should be written lightly.

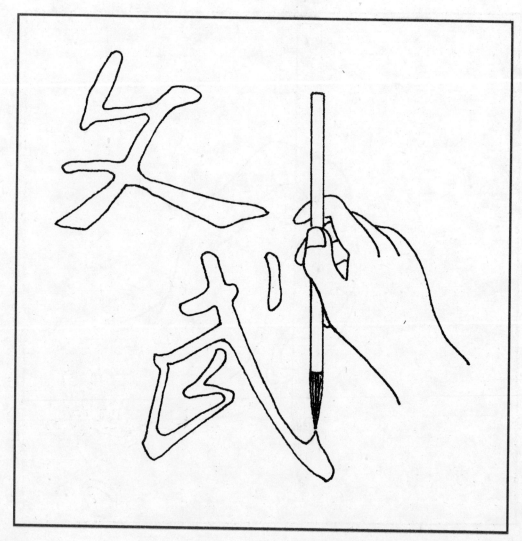

Chapter III   Strokes

A single movement of the brush is commonly known as one stroke. One who wants to write good calligraphy must learn to write strokes well.

1. Basic Strokes

There are eight kinds of basic strokes: horizontal, vertical, left-falling, right-falling, hooking, rising and cornering strokes and dots.

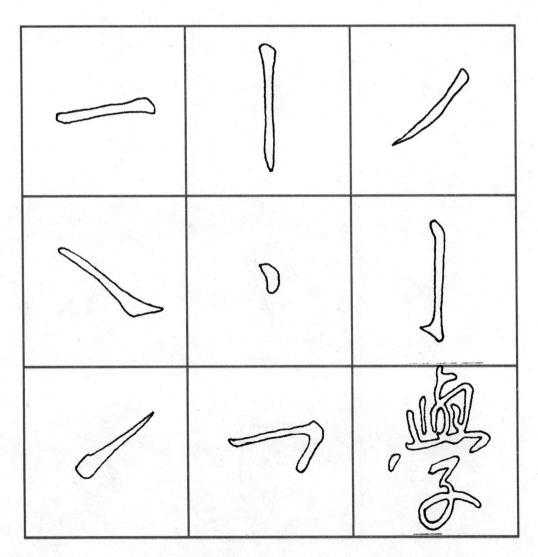

2. Complex Strokes

The strokes of Chinese characters fall into two parts: basic and complex strokes. A complex stroke consists of two to three basic strokes. After one has learnt how to write eight kinds of basic strokes, one should continue to practice complex strokes.

There are several dozens kinds of complex strokes, including the following eight kinds: left falling-cornering-cornering, vertical-cornering-cornering, horizontal-left falling-bending-hooking, horizontal-cornering-left falling, horizontal-cornering-left bending-hooking, horizontal-cornering-right bending-hooking, vertical-cornering-horizontal and horizontal-cornering-vertical-hooking strokes.

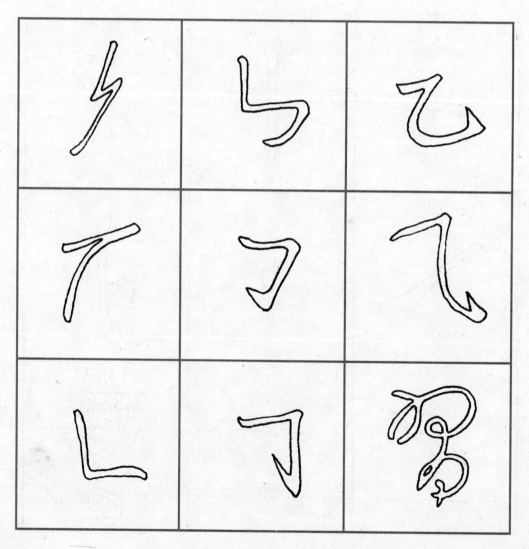

3. Changes of Strokes

Different horizontal strokes		

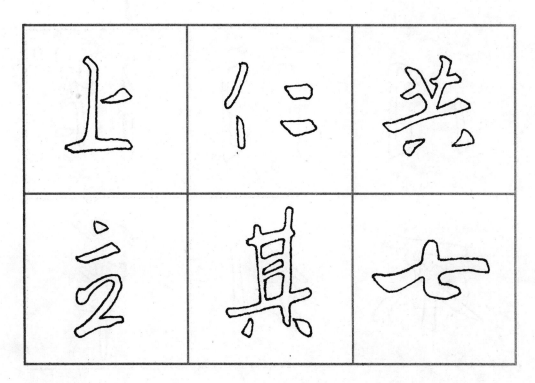

Different vertical
strokes

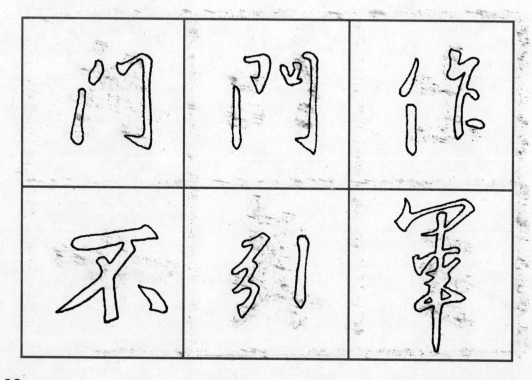

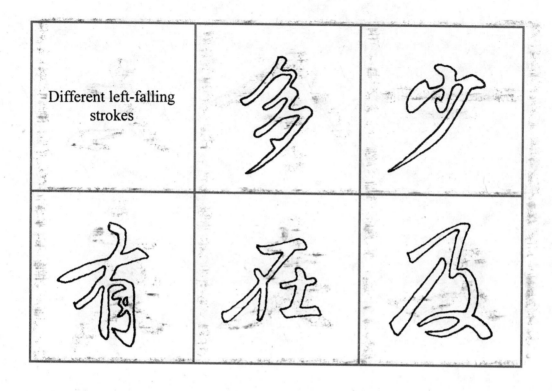

Different left-falling strokes

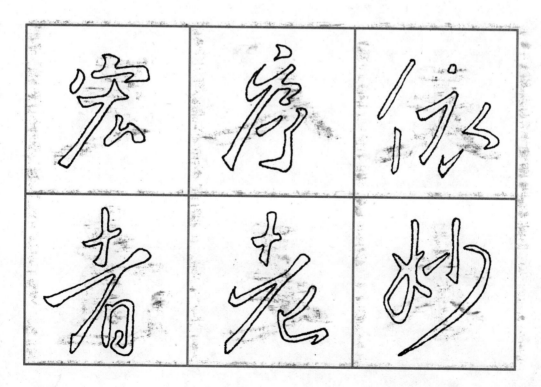

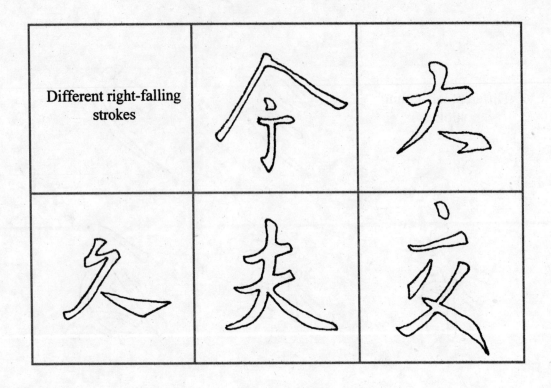

Different right-falling
strokes

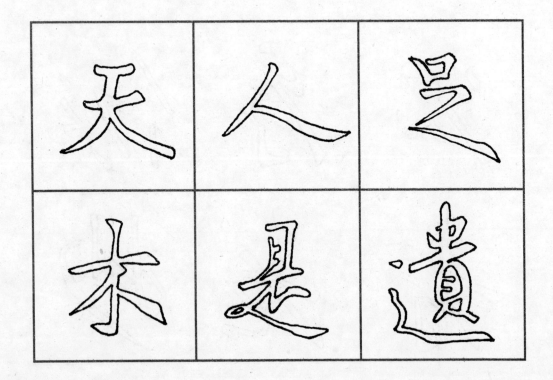

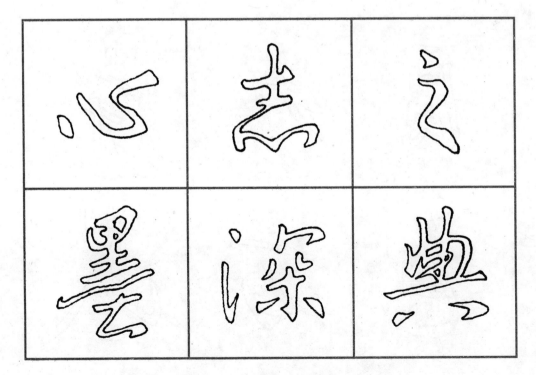

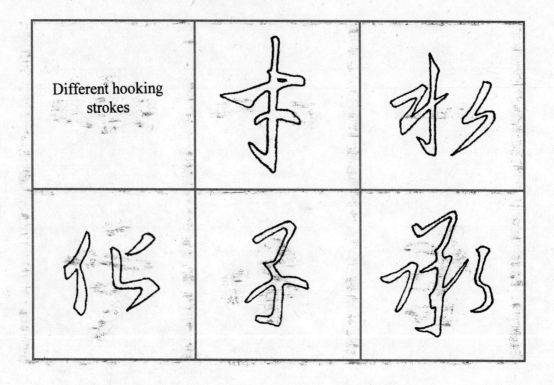

Different hooking strokes

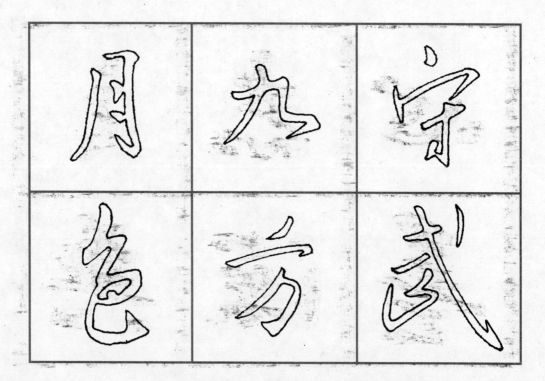

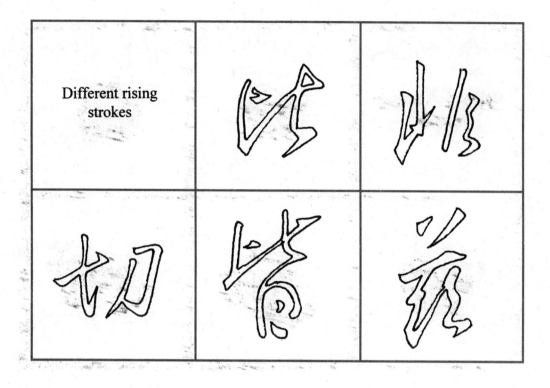

Different rising strokes

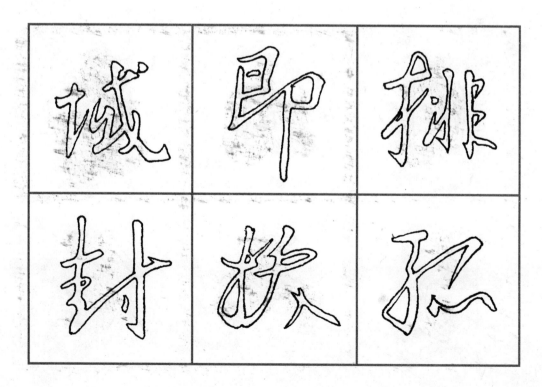

Different cornering strokes		

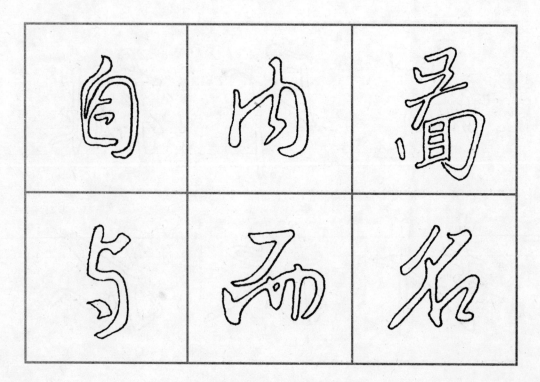

4. Order of Strokes

First horizontal, then vertical		

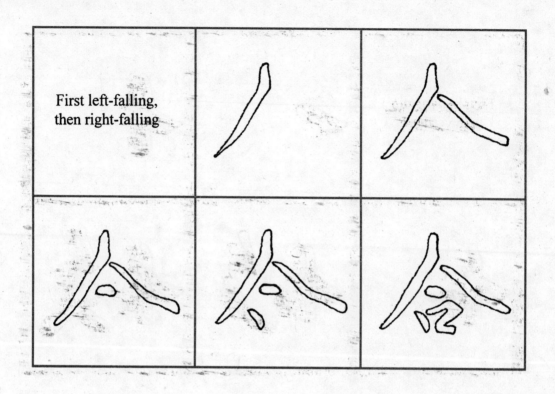

First left-falling, then right-falling

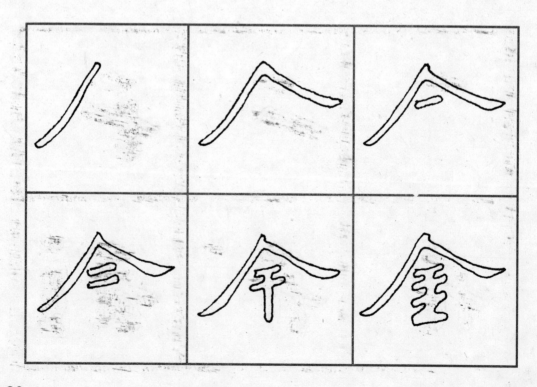

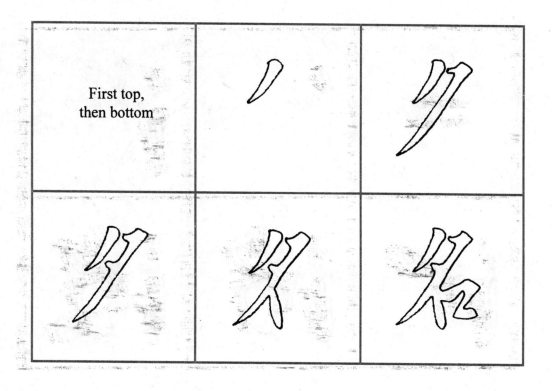

First top,
then bottom

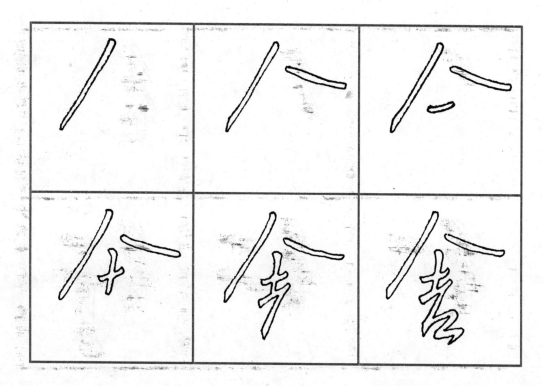

First left,
then right

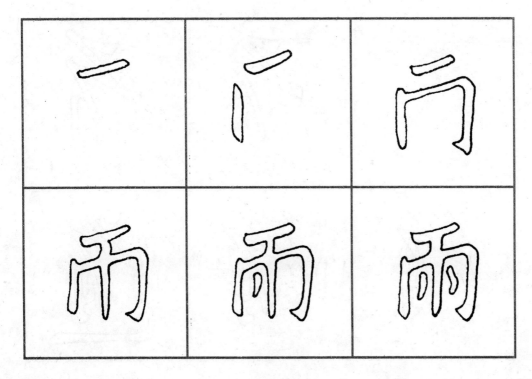

First outside,
then inside

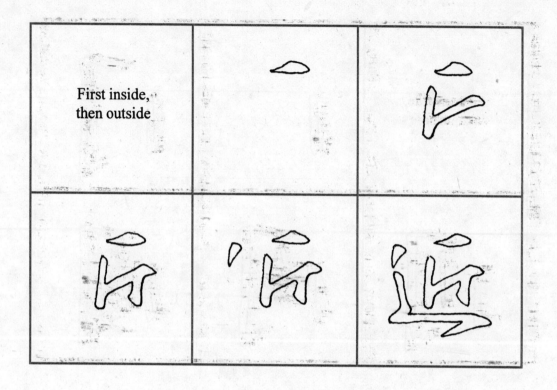

First inside,
then outside

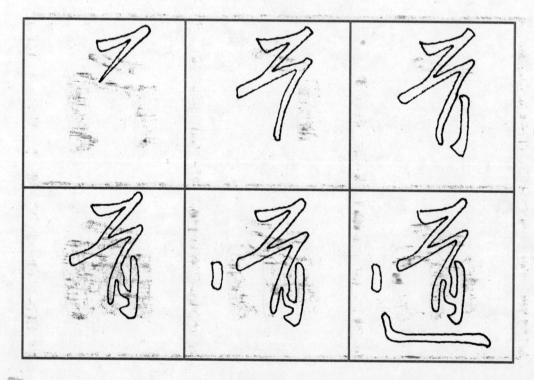

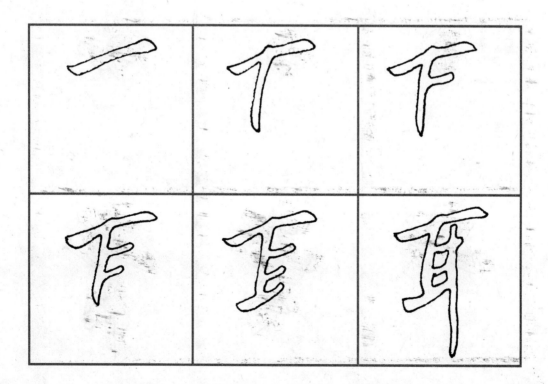

"Let him come in, then close the door."

| First center, then sides | 丨 | 业 |
| 业 | 少 | 光 |

| 丨 | ㇇ | 艹 |
| 去 | 当 | 当 |

Chapter IV　Radicals

　　Side components are the main parts composing compound-element characters. The characters with the same side component belong to the same radical.

　　More than 90 percent of Chinese characters are compound-element characters. The number of characters with the same side component varies from several dozens to several hundred. For instance, there are nearly 600 Chinese characters with the side component of 氵. So if one can write one side component well, it will help in writing well many Chinese characters with the same side component. However, while writing, one must pay attention to the changes of side components, which will be explained later.

　　The radicals are divided into the character's head, character's bottom, left component, right component and character's frame.

1. Character's Head

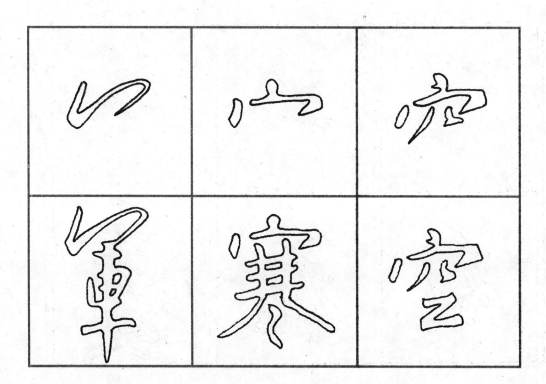

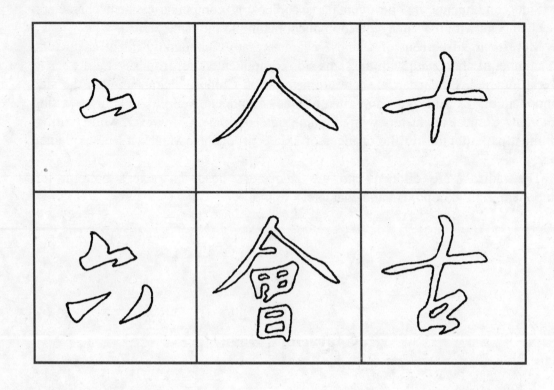

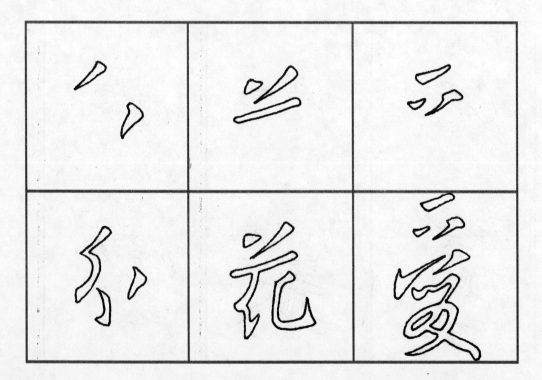

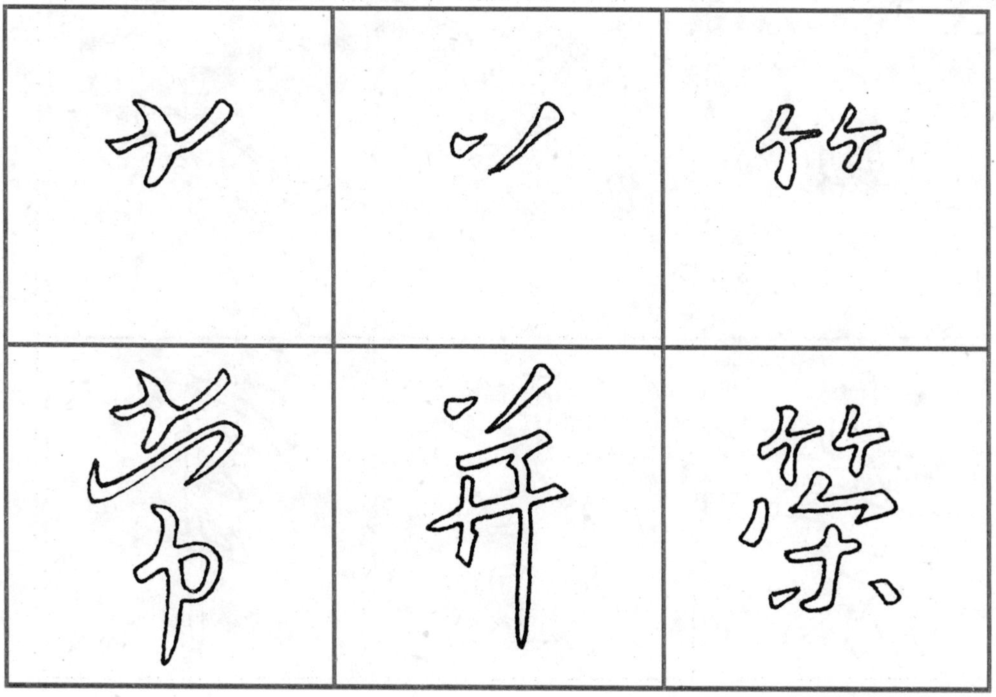

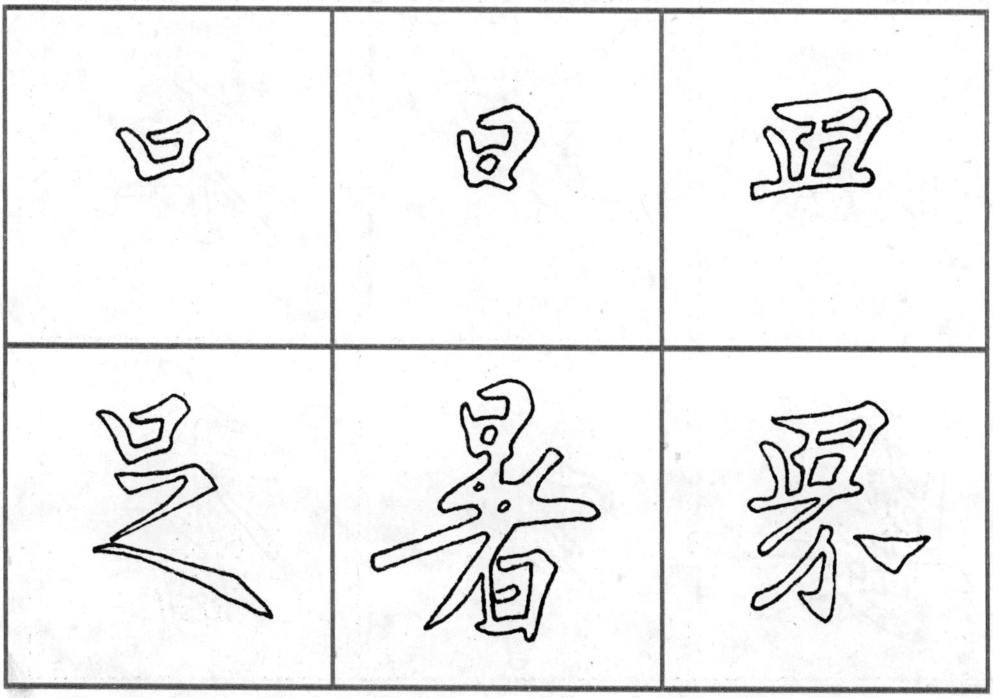

丷	八	竹
节	并	筞

口	日	四
旦	署	累

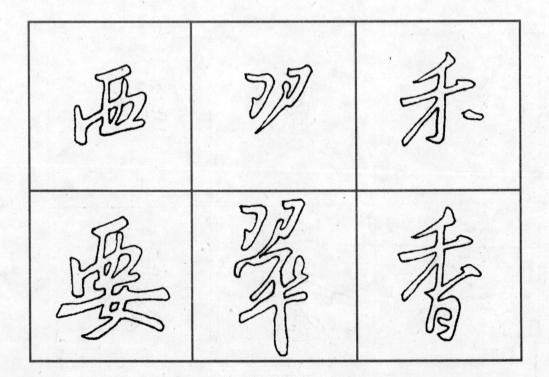

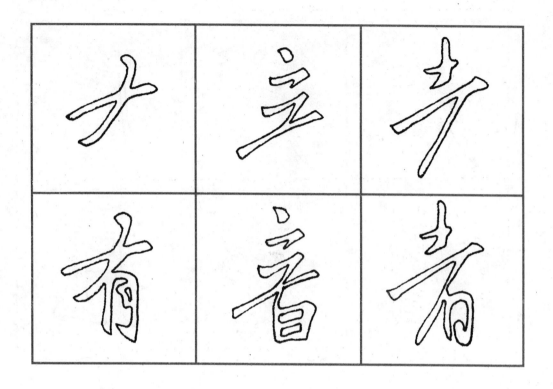

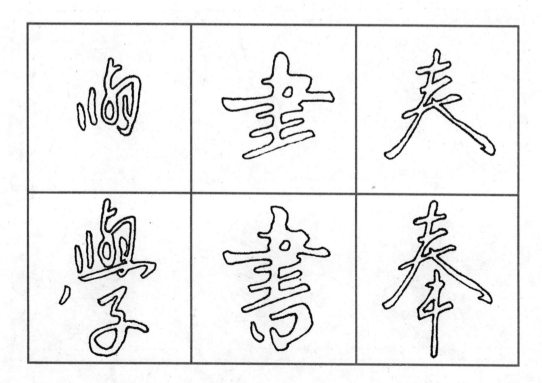

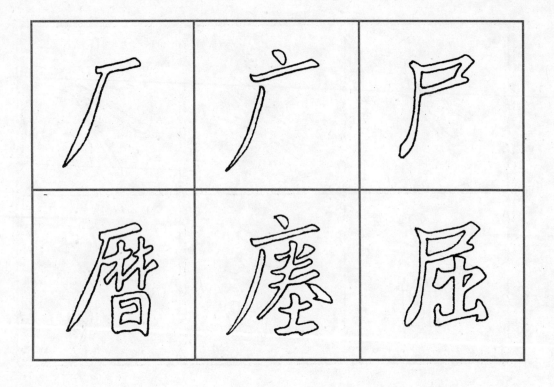

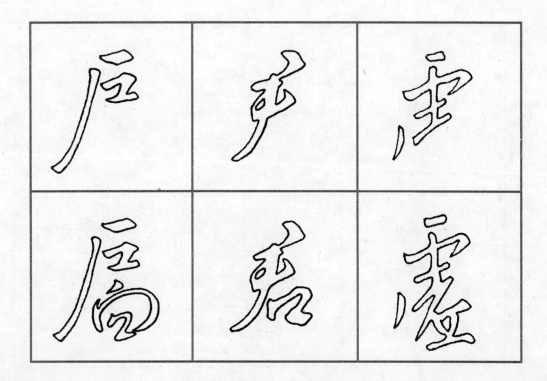

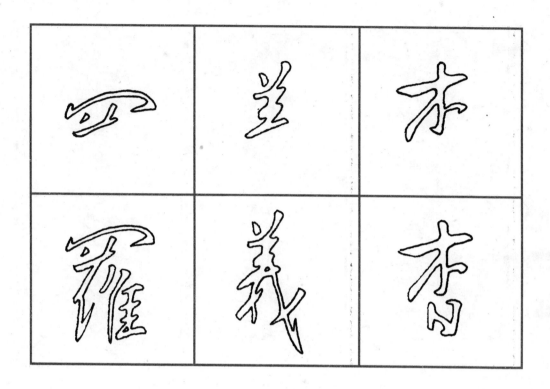

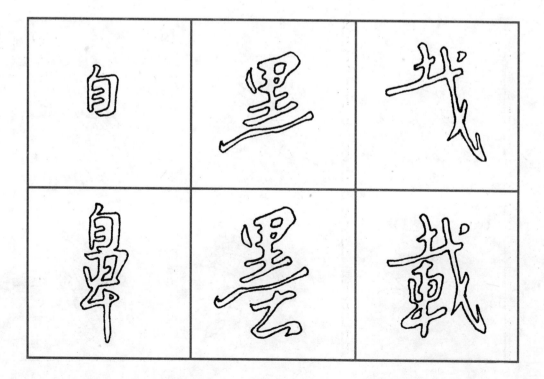

山	土	求
岳	基	栗

衣	禾	刀
製	繁	勢

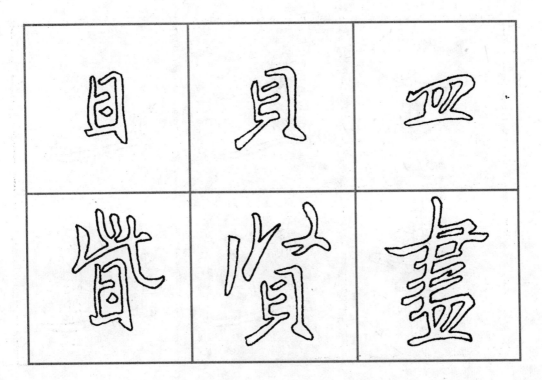

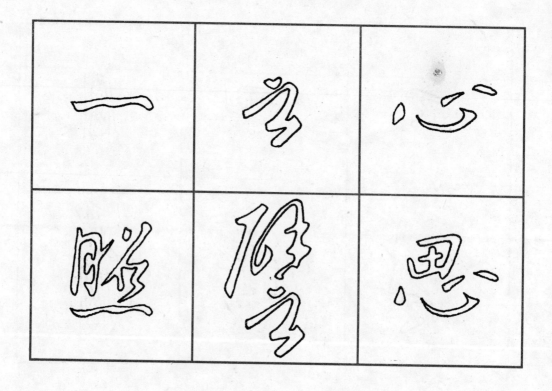

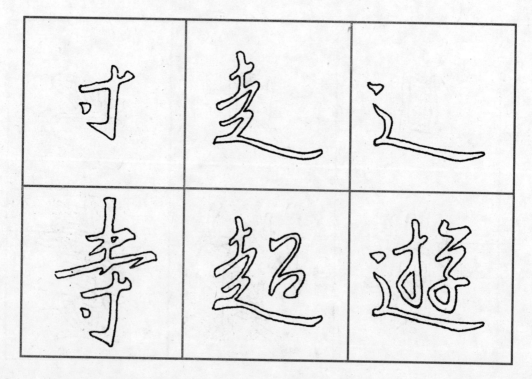

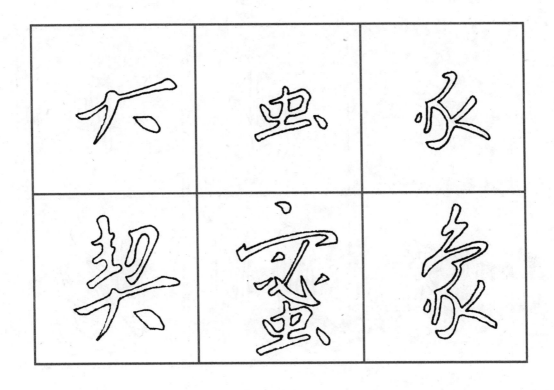

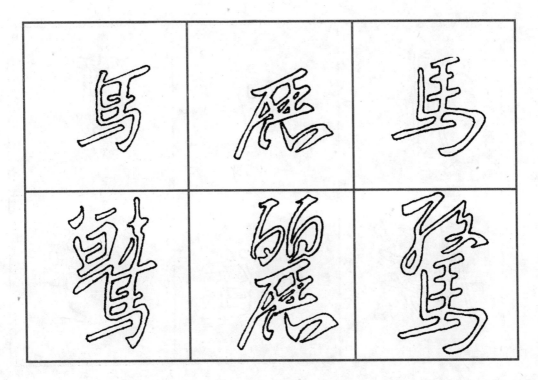

3. Left Component

心	卩	日
呪	卽	嶢

月	田	玉
朕	略	理

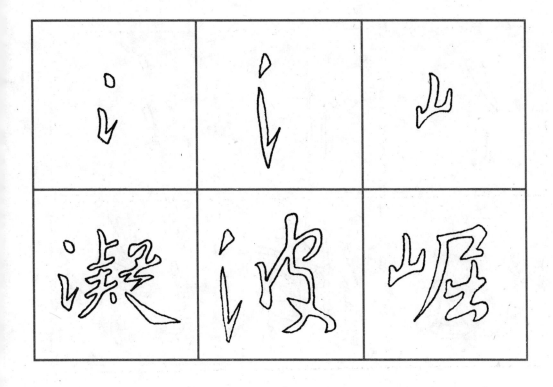

凝 波 崛

七 金 扶

城 鏡 煙

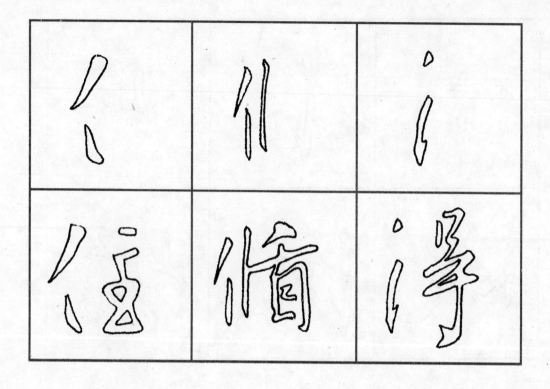

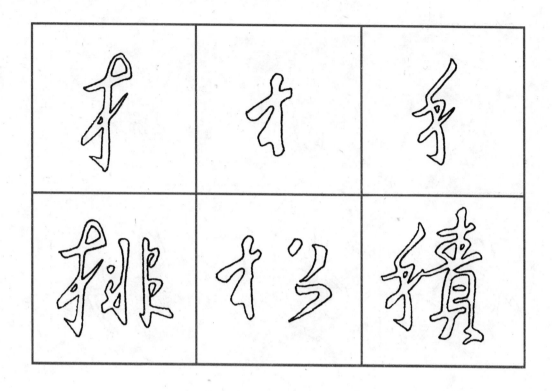

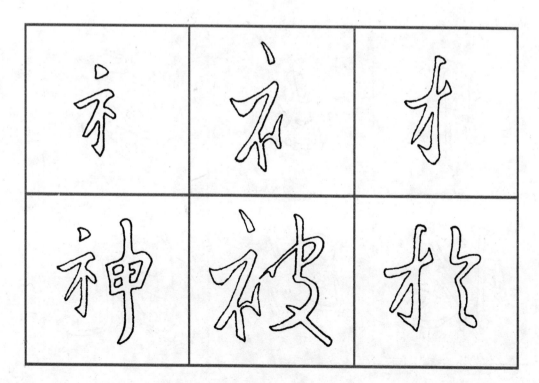

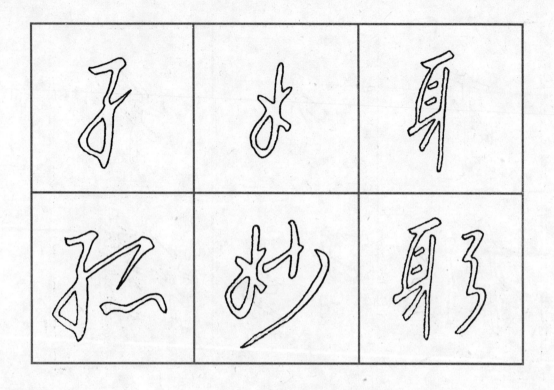

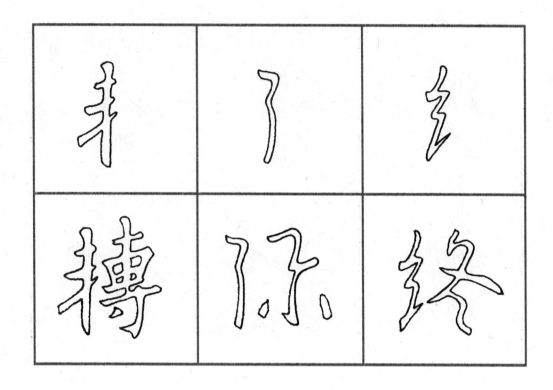

| 屯 | 牟 | 半 |
| 虬 | 犕 | 物 |

| 多 | 馬 | 牛 |
| 貂 | 駃 | 特 |

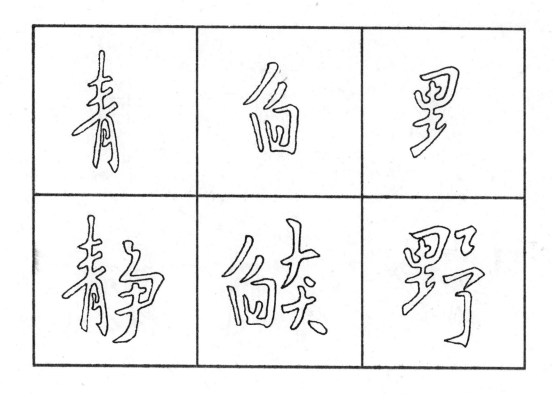

青　伯　罢
静　峡　野

臣　丰　弄
歸　輝　務

4. Right Component

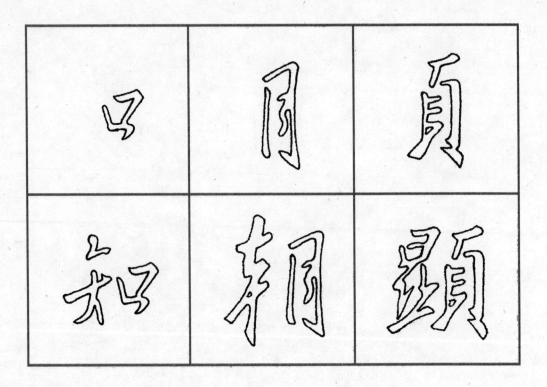

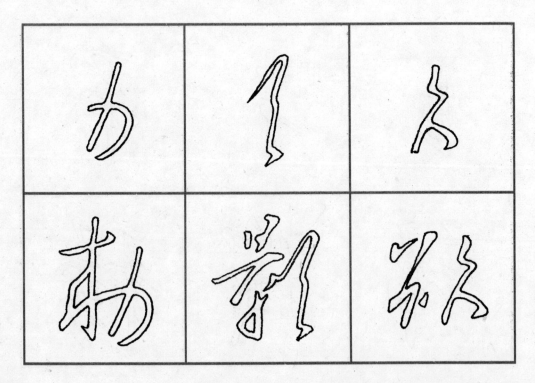

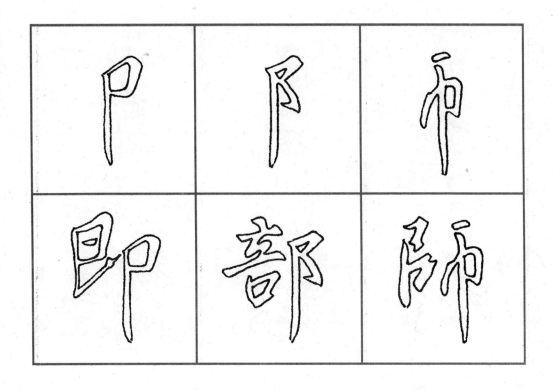

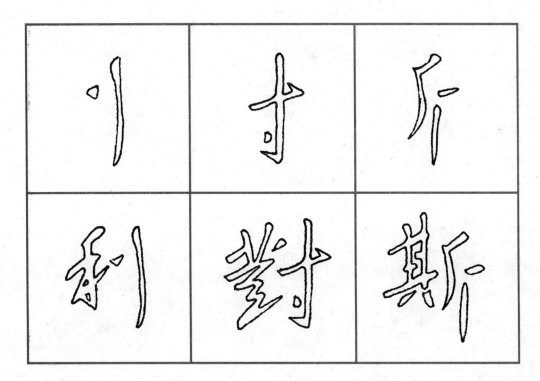

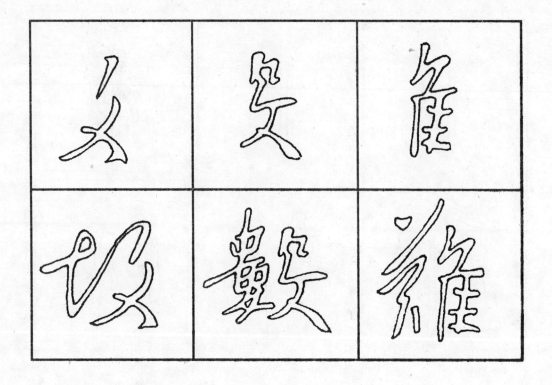

5. Character's Frame

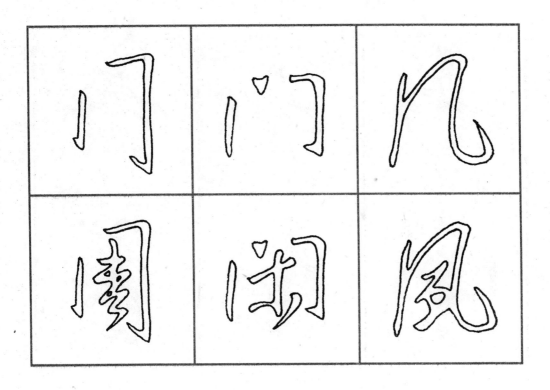

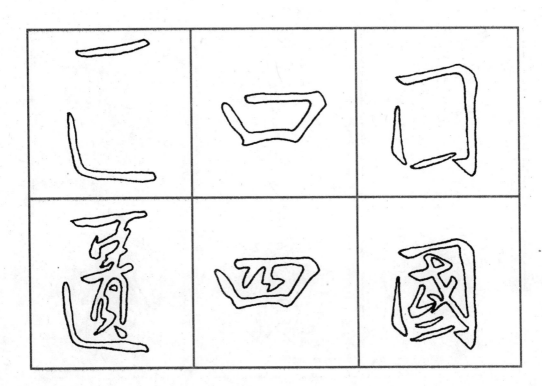

6. Changes

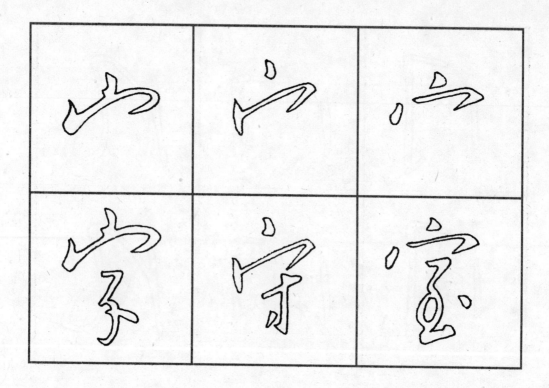

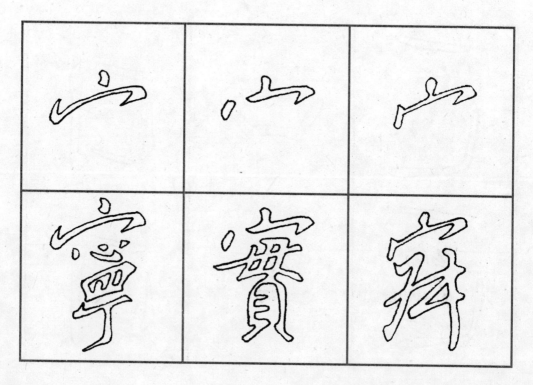

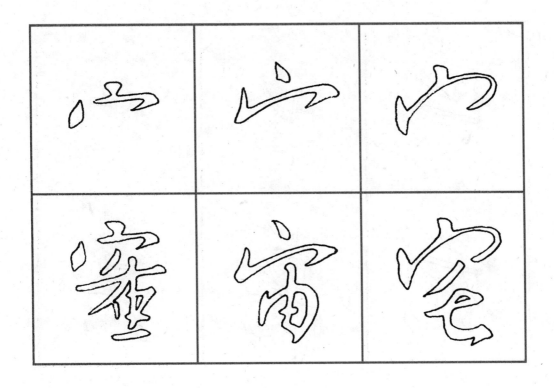

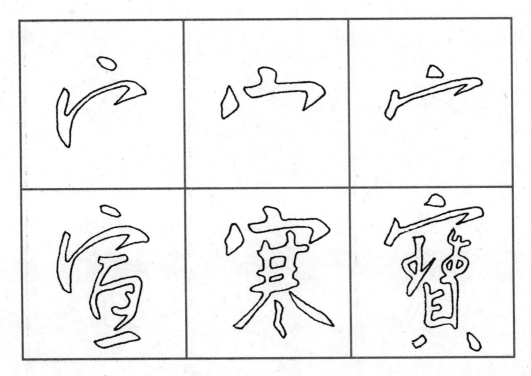

兰 小 心

花 萬 莫

分 兰 心

茂 荷 業

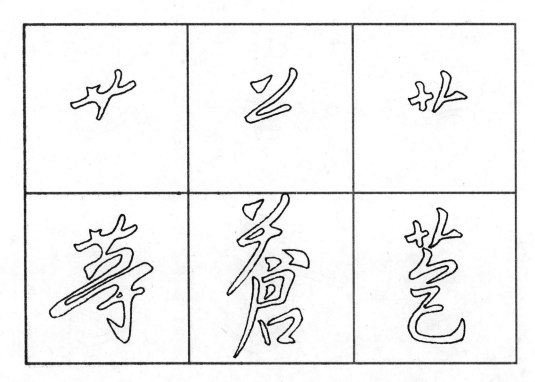

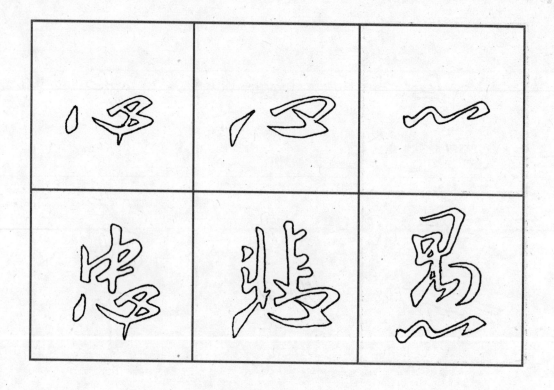

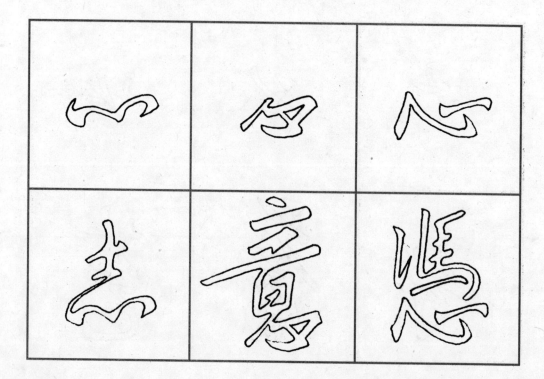

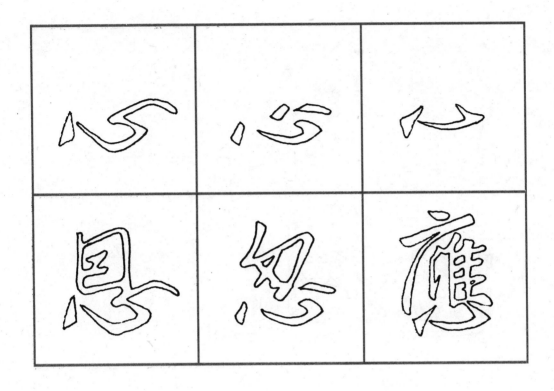

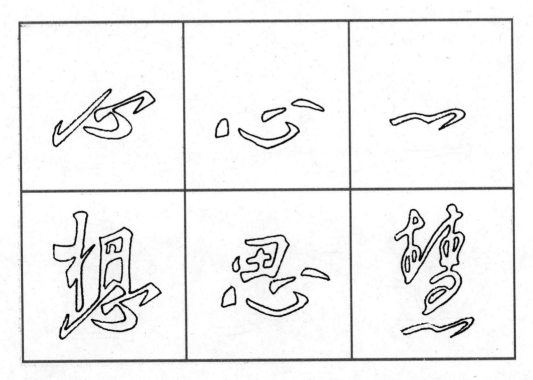

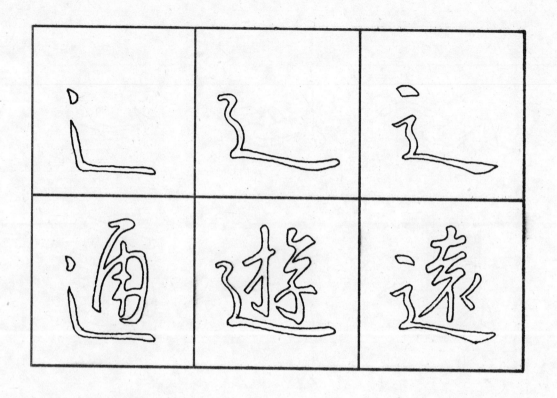

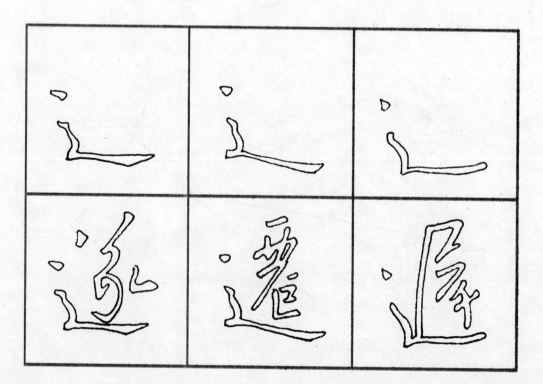

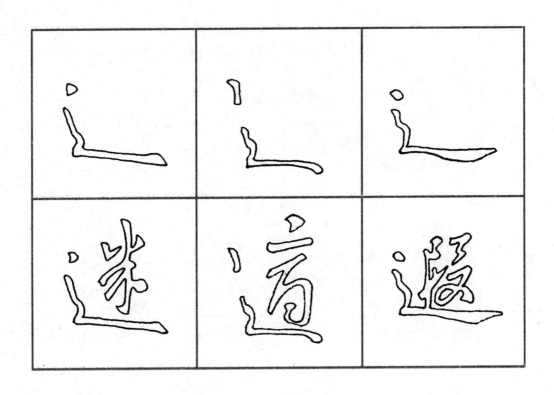

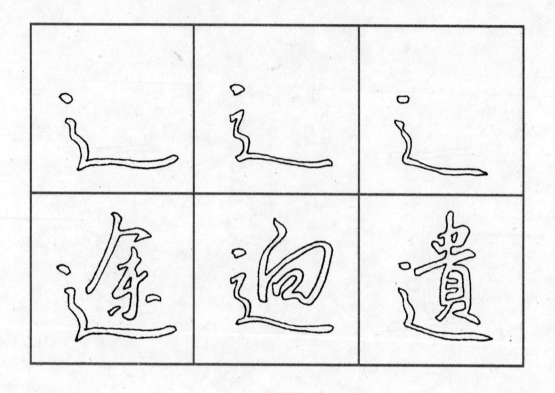

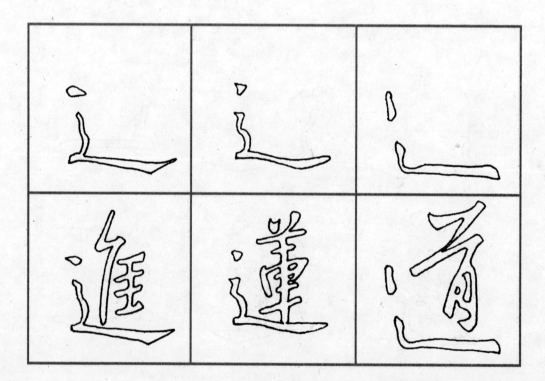

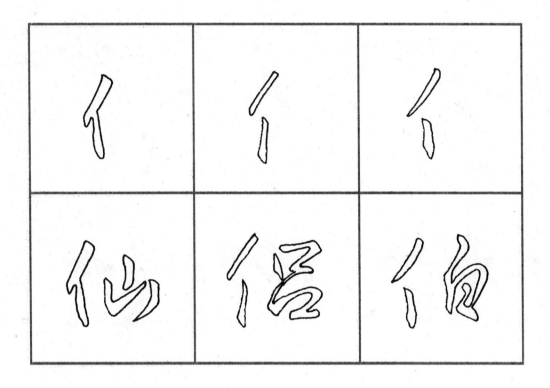

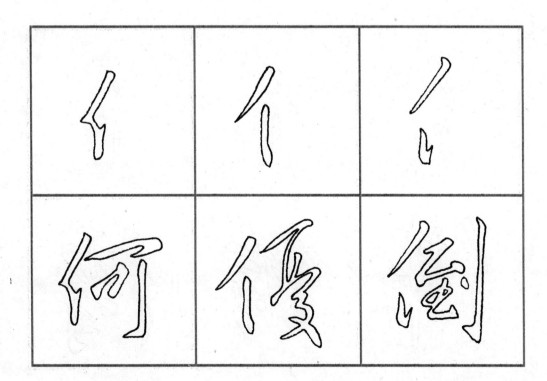

亻	亻	亻
俗	仰	使

亻	亻	亻
佛	備	傳

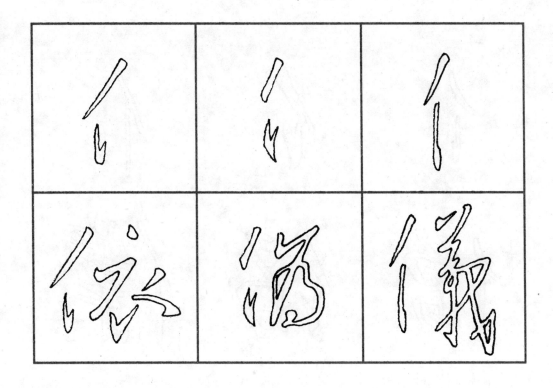

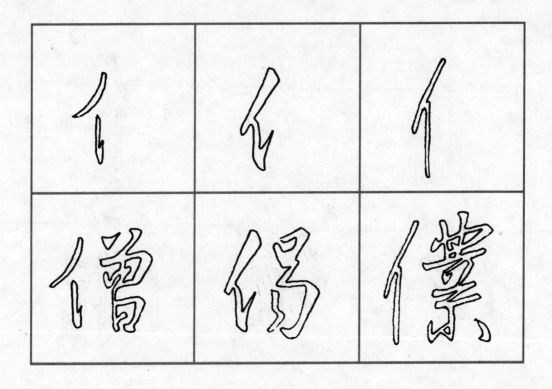

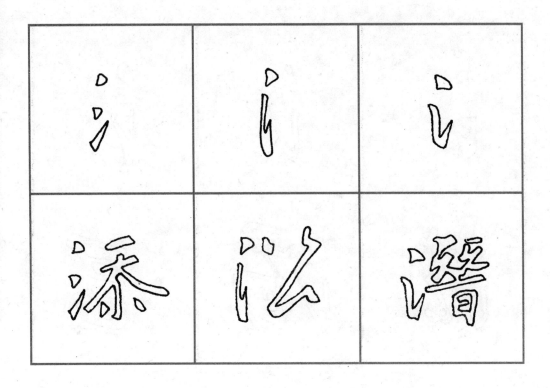

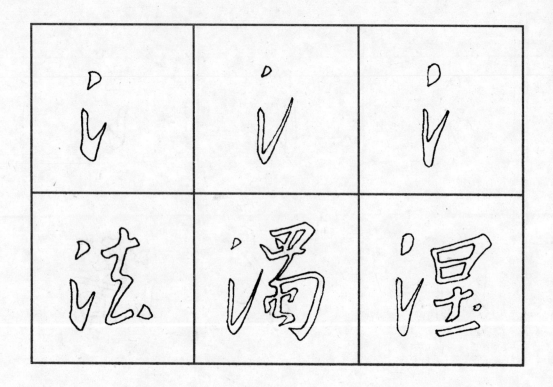

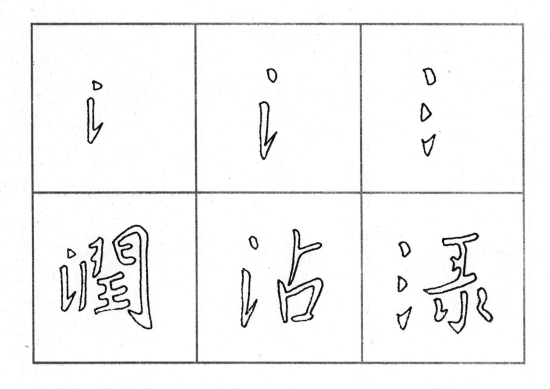

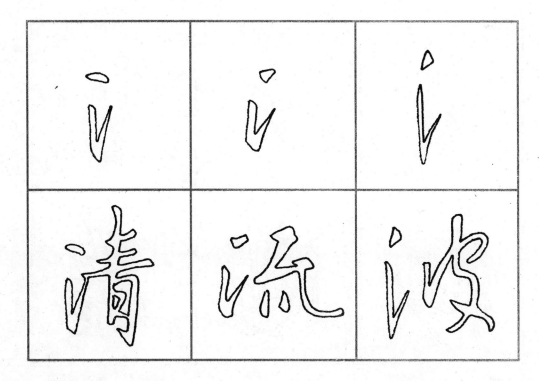

⺡	⻌	⺡
洗	洞	滿

⺡	⺡	⺡
澤	湛	濁

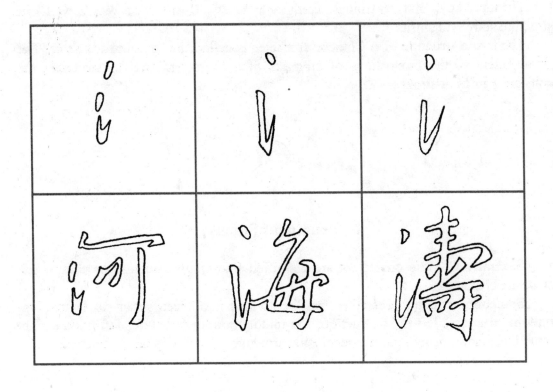

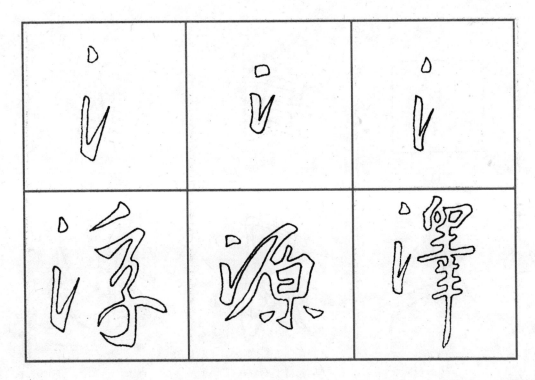

Chapter V   Structure

The three key points to Chinese calligraphy are: well-written strokes, a well-knit structure and vivid spirits.

The frame structure of a Chinese character is called the structure for short. The frame refers to the proportions of all parts of a character; and the structure, the consisting rules of strokes.

1. Structural Forms

Generally Chinese characters are classified into single-structure or compound-structure characters.

Compound-structure characters can be divided into seven structural forms: top-bottom structure, left-right structure, top-middle-bottom structure, left-middle-right structure, semi-closing structure, enclosing structure and 品-character structure.

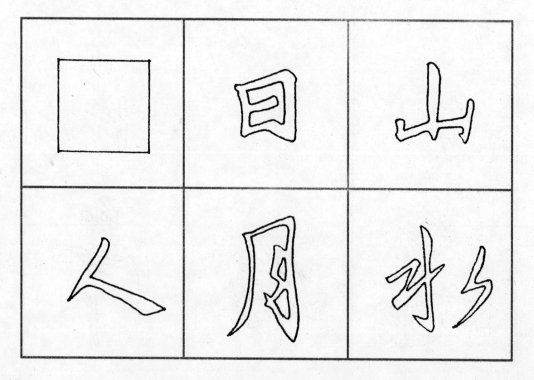

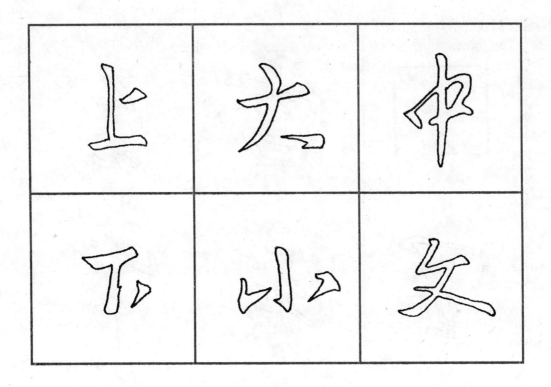

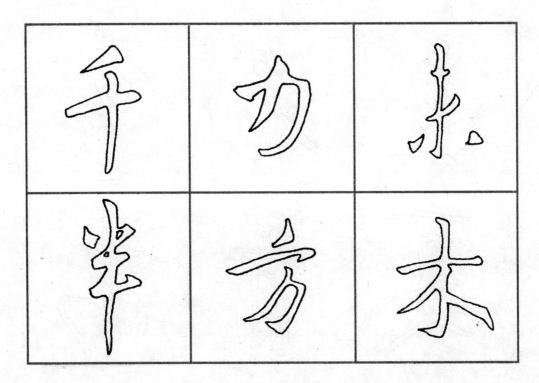

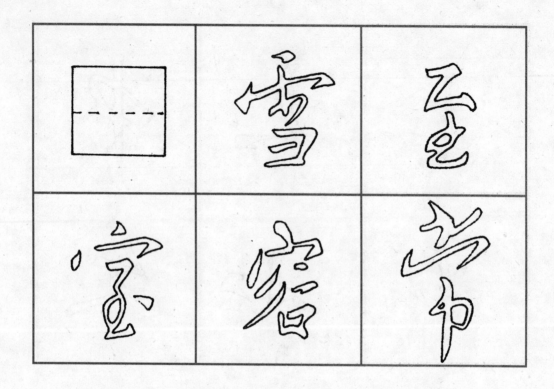

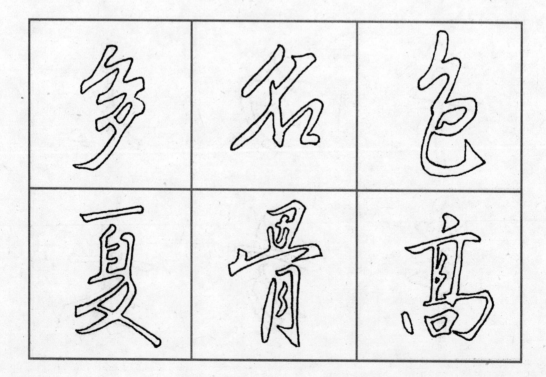

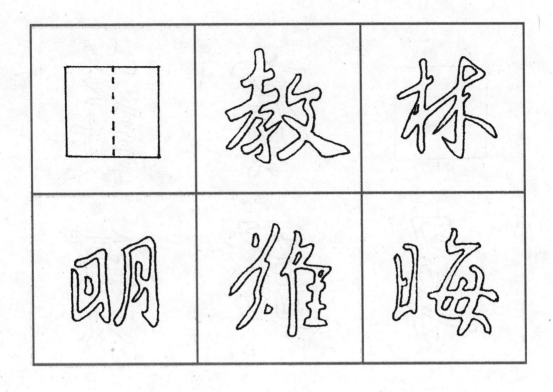

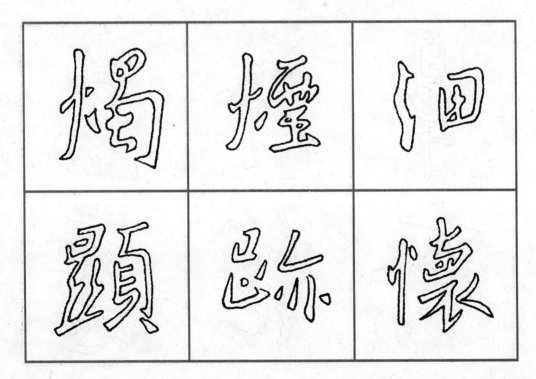

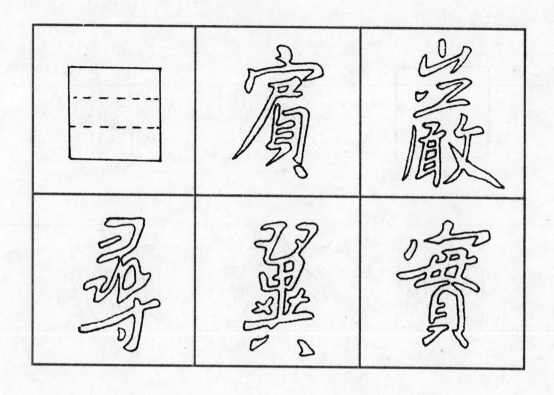

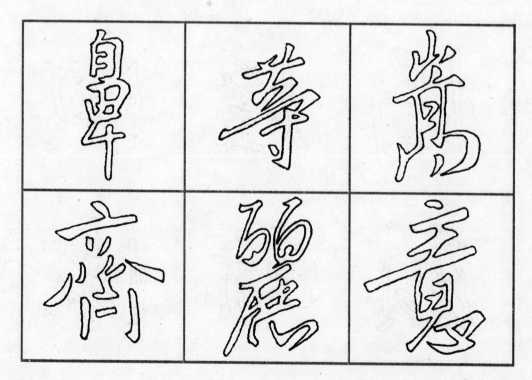

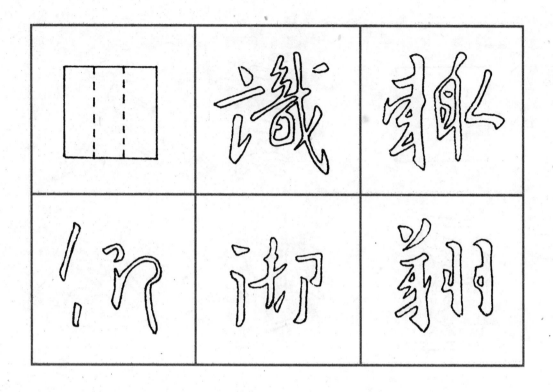

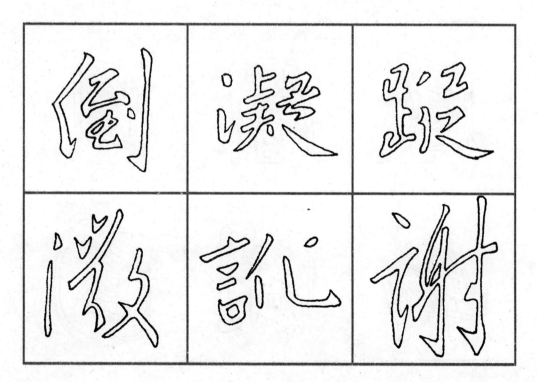

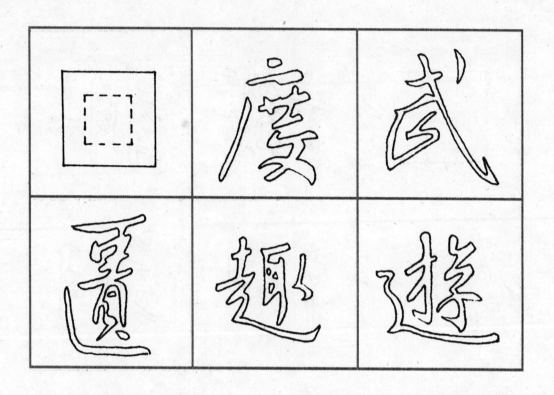

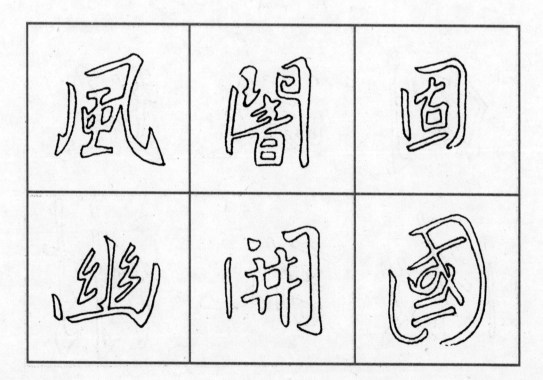

2. Structural Proportions

The structural proportion means the location and size of each part of a character. In a same structural form, different proportions exist among various parts of a character in terms of height, width, size and length. For instance, as to the top-bottom structure, now the top and bottom parts are same in size; now the top is larger than the bottom; and now the top is smaller than the bottom. With regard to the semi-closing structure, now the top part encloses the bottom part; now the bottom part encloses the top part; now the left part encloses the right part; and now the right part encloses the left part. Of course the proportions are not unalterable. People may refer to the structural proportions flexibly, and write a character in different structural forms.

If one has a good command of the structural proportion, one may write beautiful Chinese characters no matter how many strokes a character has and how complicated a character's structure is.

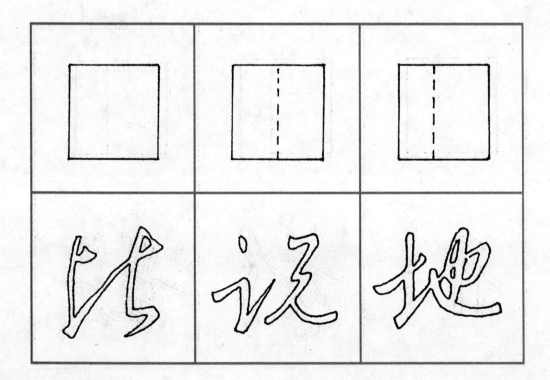

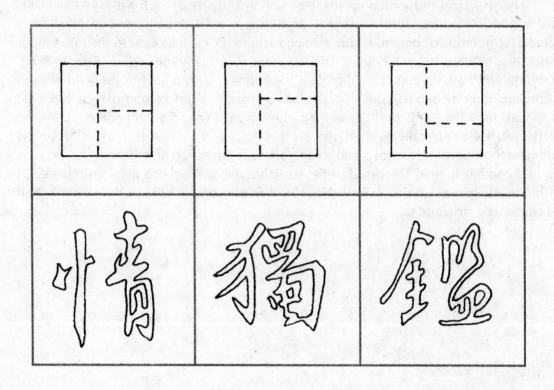

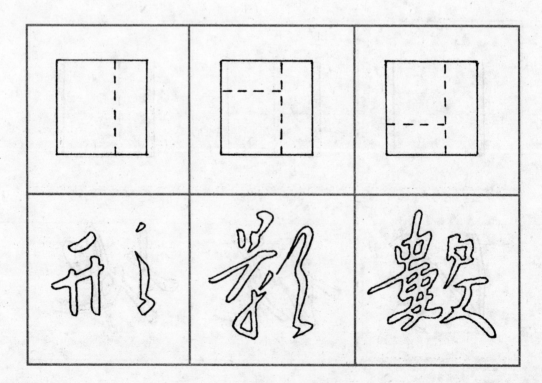

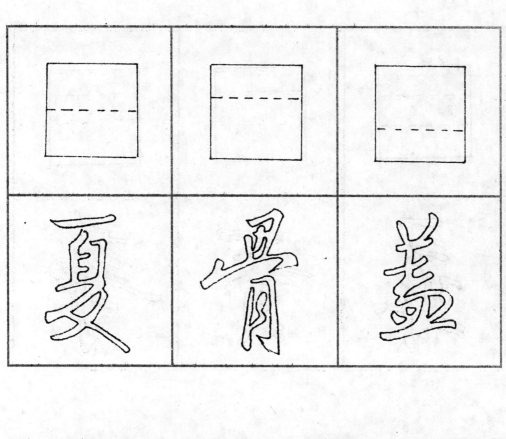

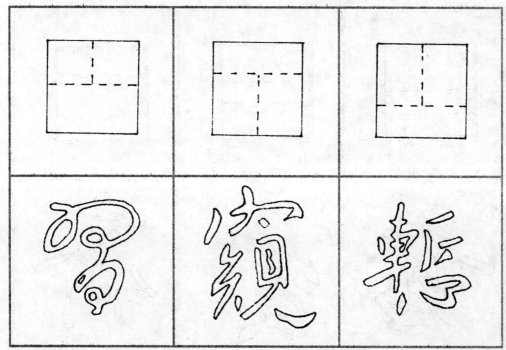

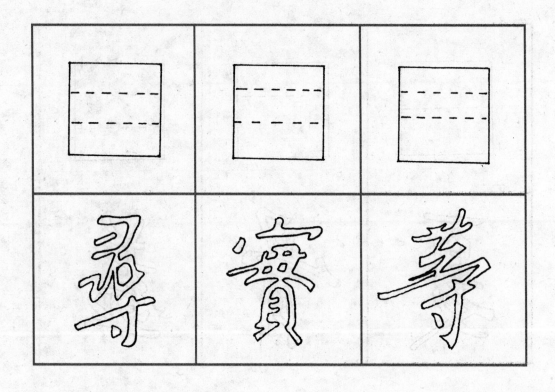

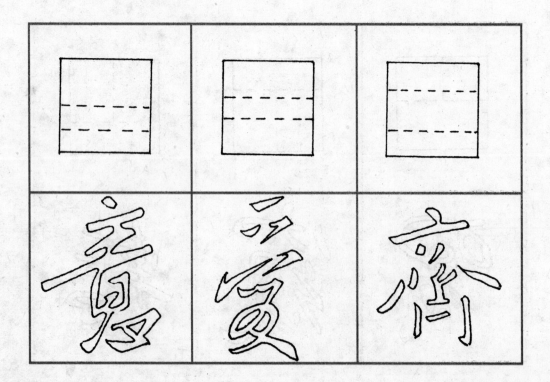

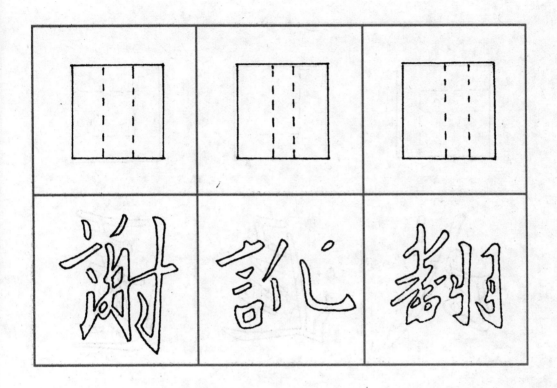

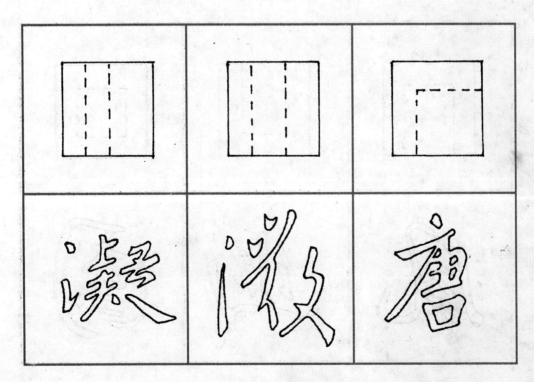

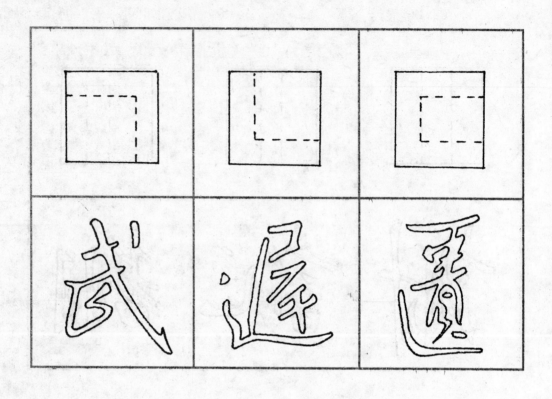

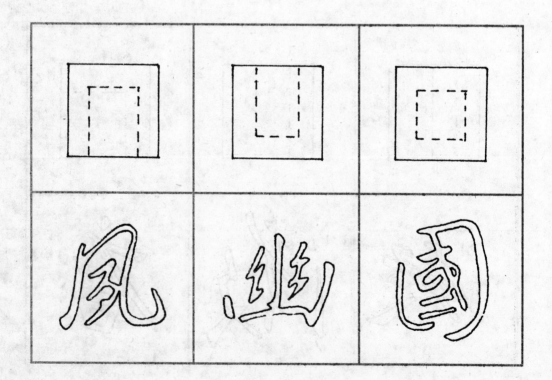

3. Outline of the Structure

Chinese characters developed from irregularly shaped inscriptions on bones or tortoise shells, rectangle seal script, and slightly deltoid-shaped official script to square regular script.

Chinese characters are known as block-style characters. But not every character is square. Many of them have developed into the shapes of circular, rhombus, triangle, trapezoid, and polygon. Even square characters vary in size. This is true of regular script as well as running script. Various changes taking place in a small block is one of the charms of Chinese calligraphy.

Understanding the outline of the structure will help us know the structure of a character as a whole. Just like drawing a sketch, a painter should first of all work out the outline of a sketch.

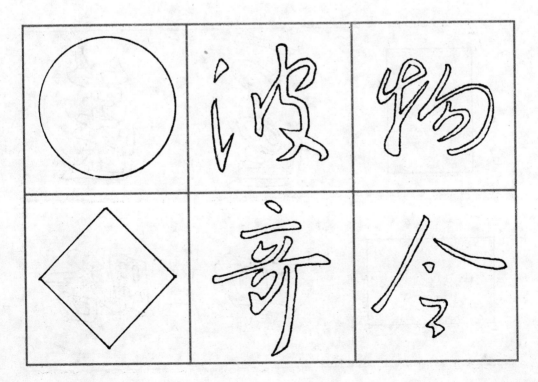

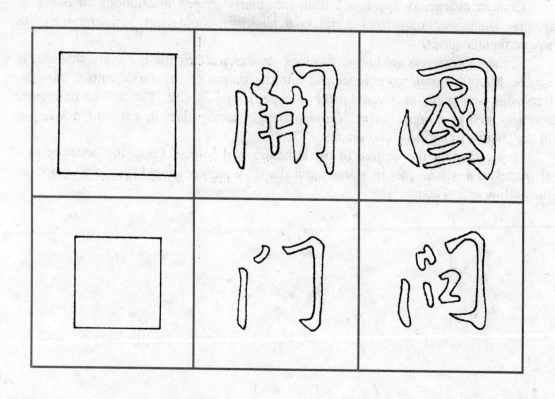

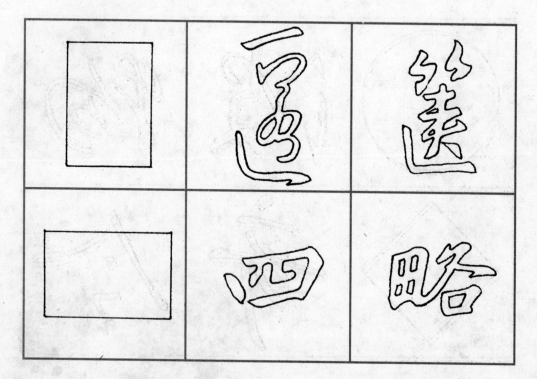

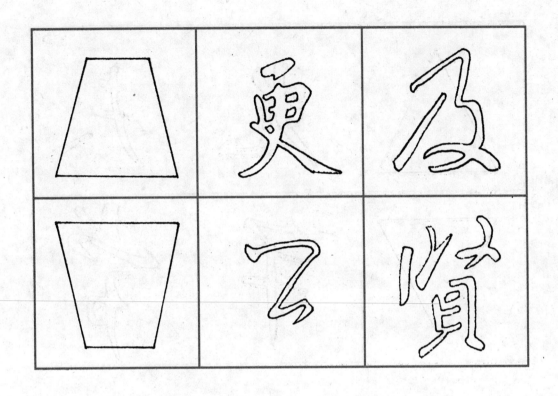

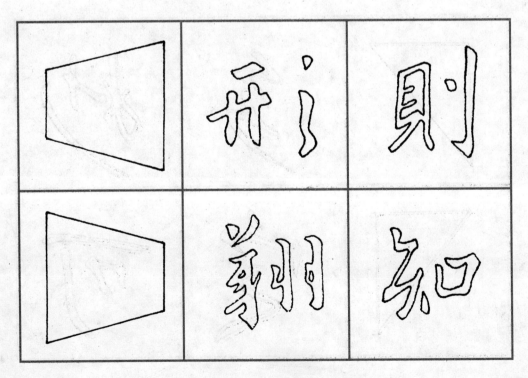

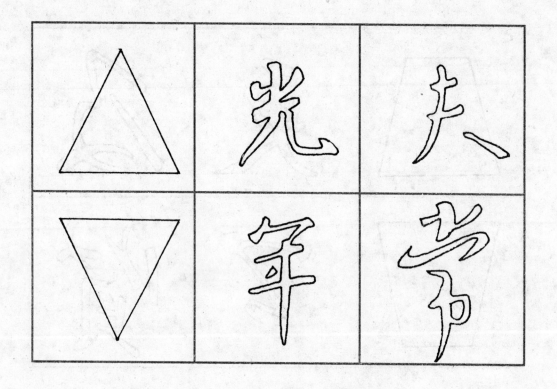

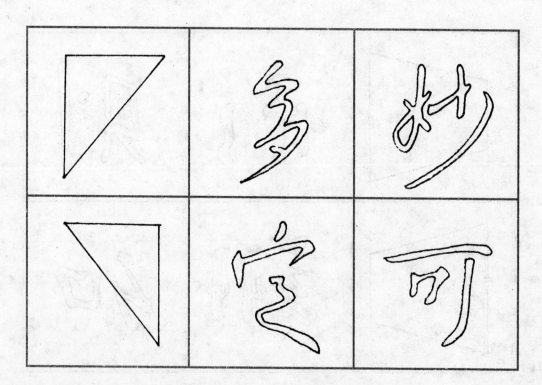

4. The Law of the Structure

While studying the structure of characters, one should not only know how the structure of a character is arranged, but also understand why the character is arranged in such a way. So a calligrapher must know the rules that must be observed in creating beautifully written characters.

Though running script is not restricted by the laws of regular script, one must abide by some laws so as to avoid writing "wild and weird" running characters as one pleases. Each of various schools of Chinese calligraphy has its own style, but each is particular about the "laws".

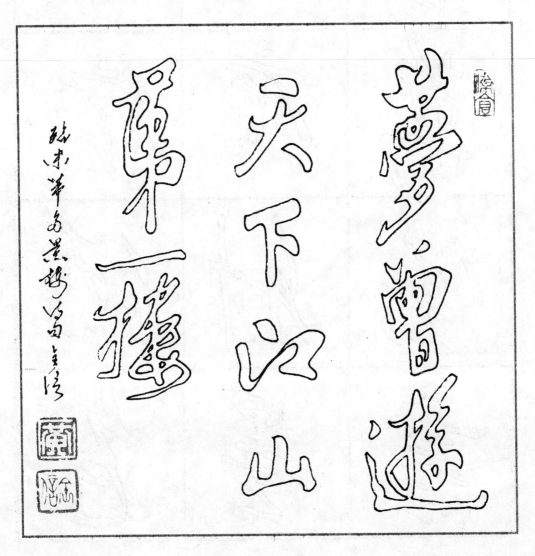

1. A Stable Center of Gravity

Beautifully shaped characters are slightly slanting and
evenly arranged, with a stable center of gravity.

秀	道	来
萬	應	室
像	射	傍
壽	里	色

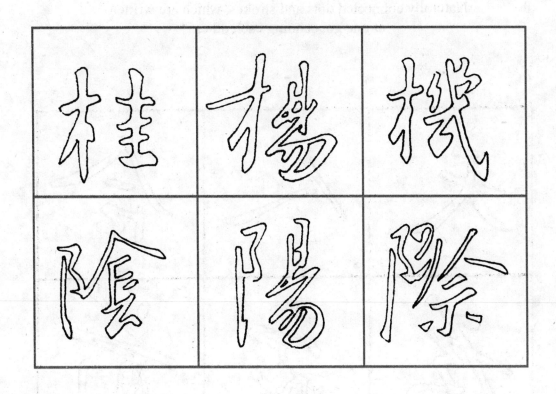

桂 楊 機
陰 陽 際

記 領 糎
鑑 顯 鏡

2. Dots and Strokes Echo Each Other

Naturally connected dots and strokes, which are written
at one go, echoing each other.

天	人	合
為	象	前
騰	坤	極
重	遊	續

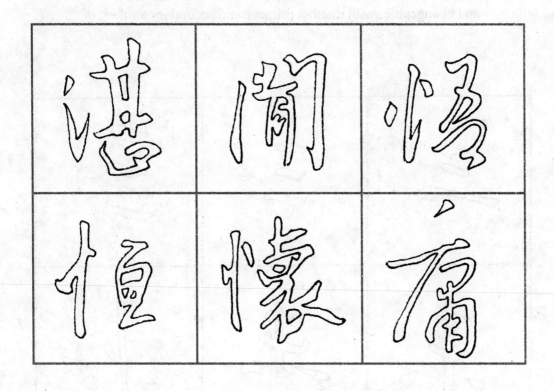

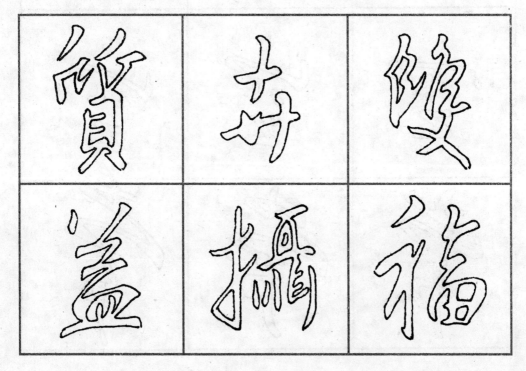

3. Unevenness and Change

Dots and strokes are placed properly. Characters are uneven and changeable, with distinct primary and secondary strokes.

三	三	三
未	未	未
空	空	空
常	常	常

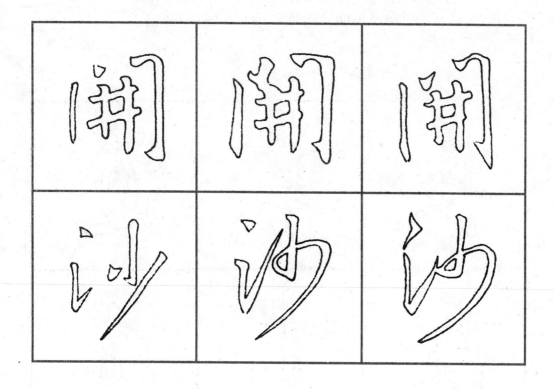

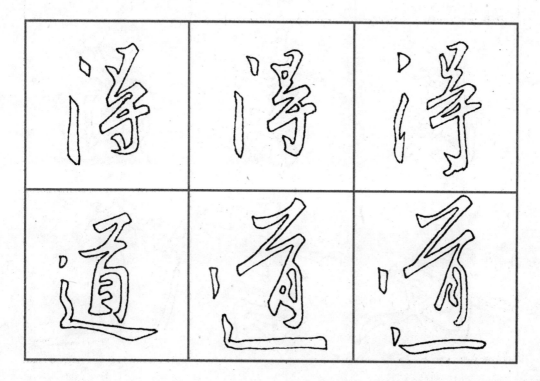

4. Coordination and Unification

Characters are evenly written, showing coordinated
strokes, a natural style and a unified posture.

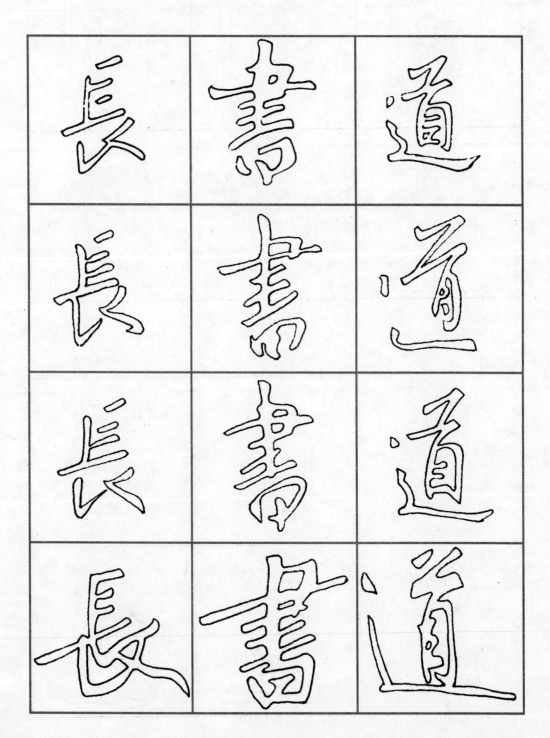

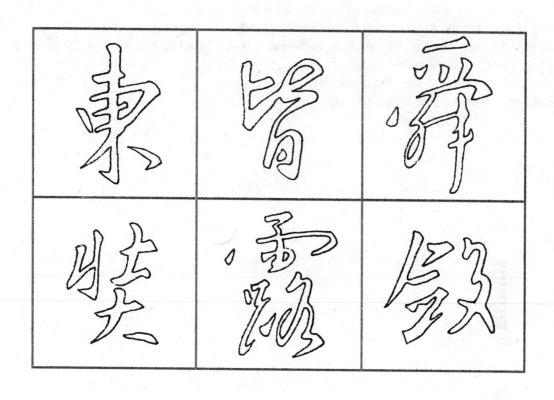

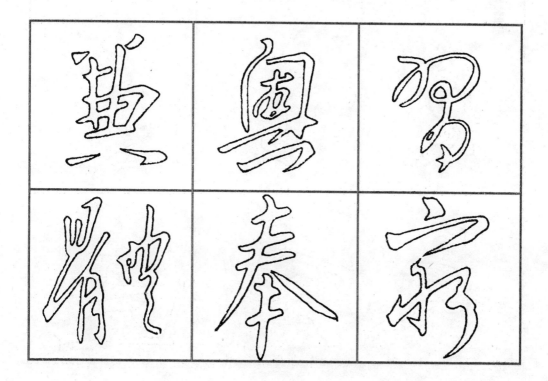

5. Changes of the Structure

Among the laws for creating beautiful Chinese calligraphy, diversification and unification are the most important. Unification depends on echo and coordination; and diversification, on contrast, such as square and round, curved and straight, thick and thin, hidden and exposed, light and heavy, slow and quick, tough and soft, dry and moist, etc. One of the important differences between the art of calligraphy and ordinary characters written with a writing brush is the various changes.

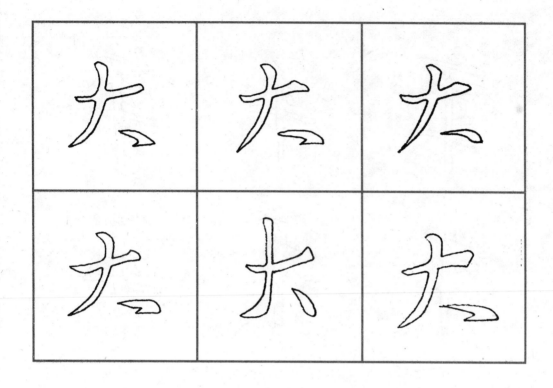

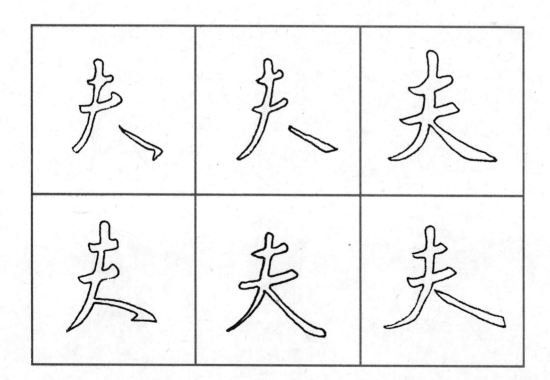

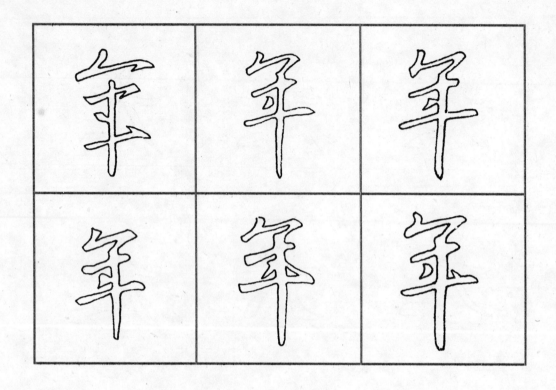

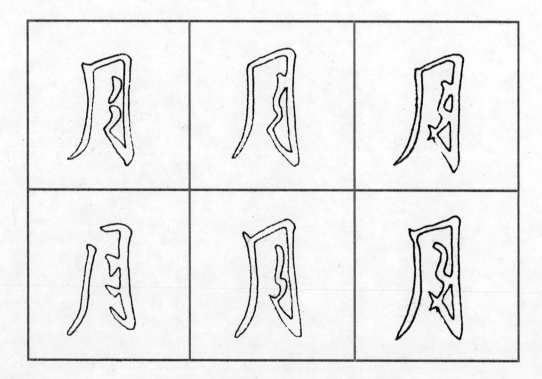

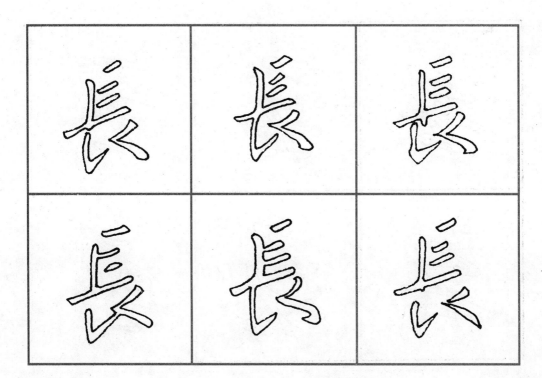

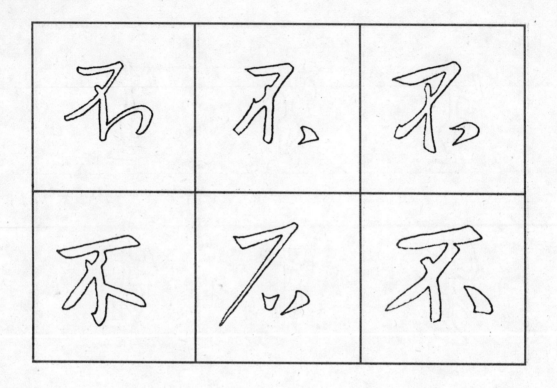

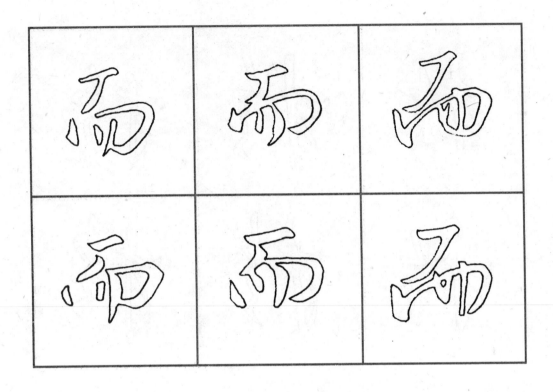

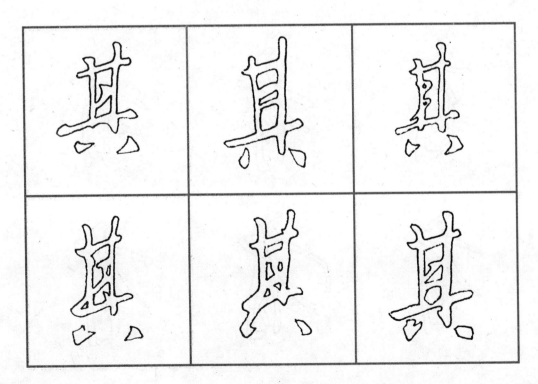

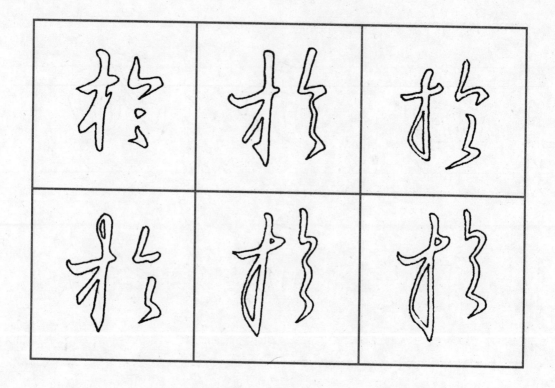

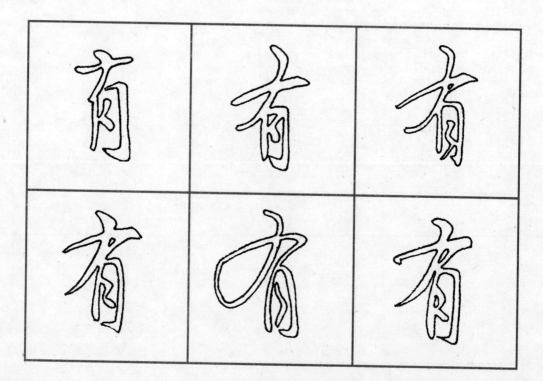

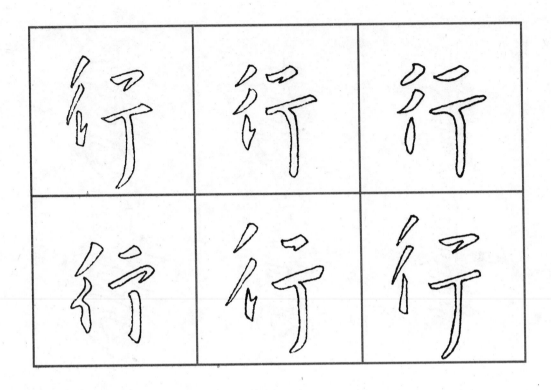

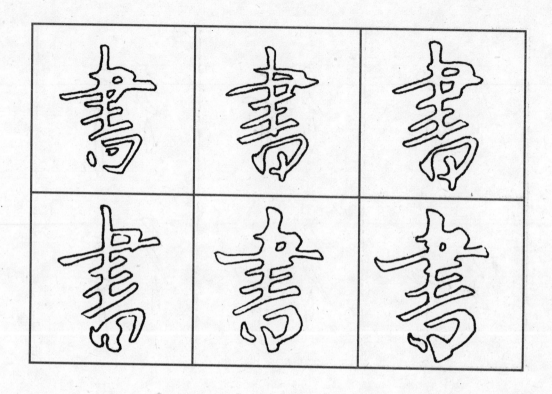

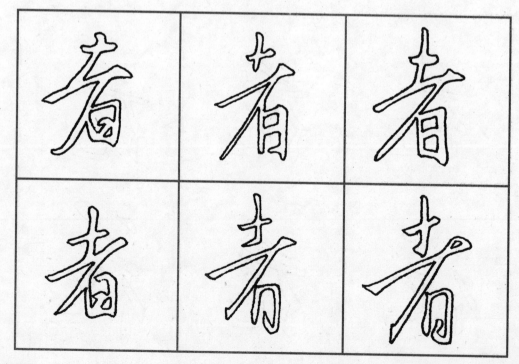

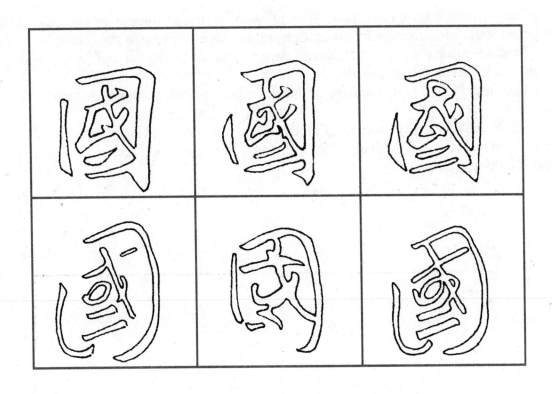

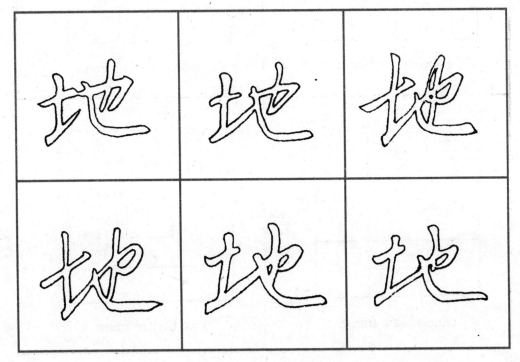

Chapter VI   Tracing and Copying

Tracing and copying are two different ways to learn Chinese calligraphy. A beginner starts with tracing Chinese calligraphy and takes copying as the mainstay.

Tracing: Place a piece of transparent paper on top of the model and trace it with brush and ink as exactly as possible.

Copying: Put the model in front of the writer and copy characters as accurately as possible.

There are many ways to copy Chinese characters: line copying, check copying, frame copying, contract copying, back copying, reciting copying, enlarging copying and shrinking copying.

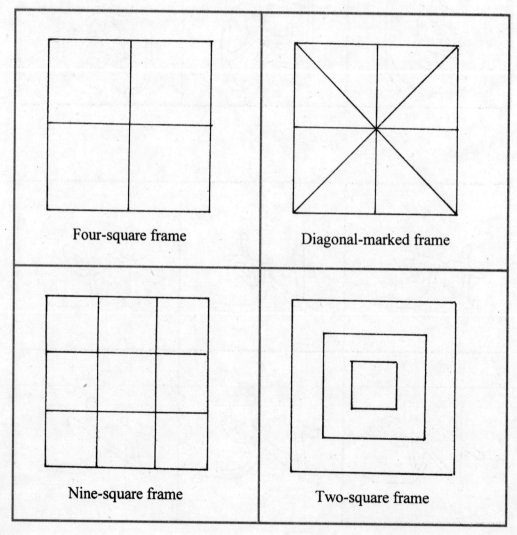

Four-square frame

Diagonal-marked frame

Nine-square frame

Two-square frame

1. Four-Square Frame

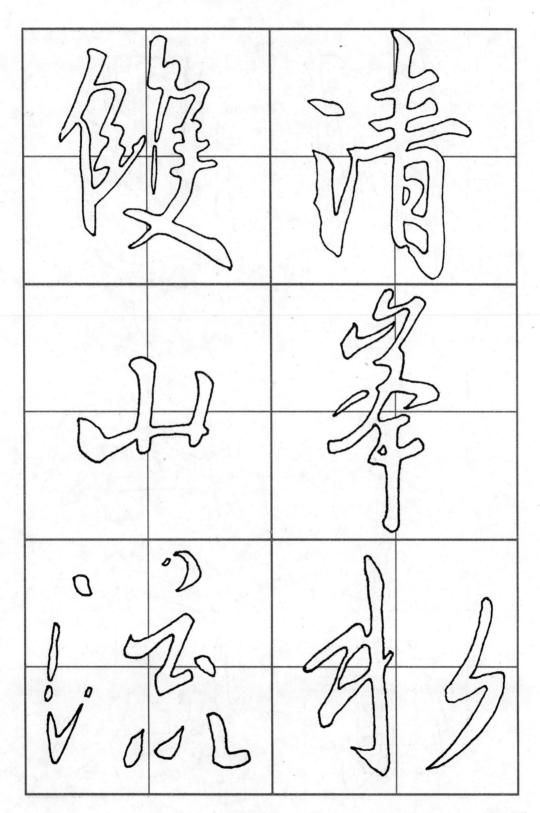

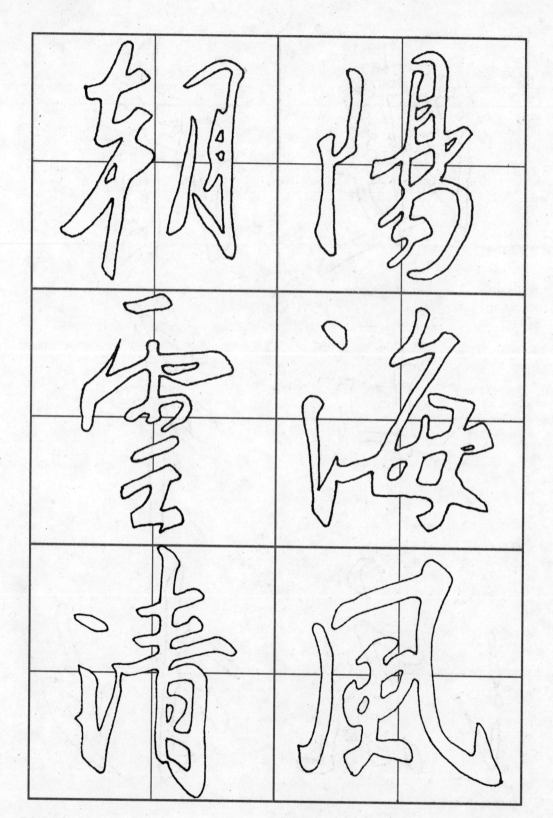

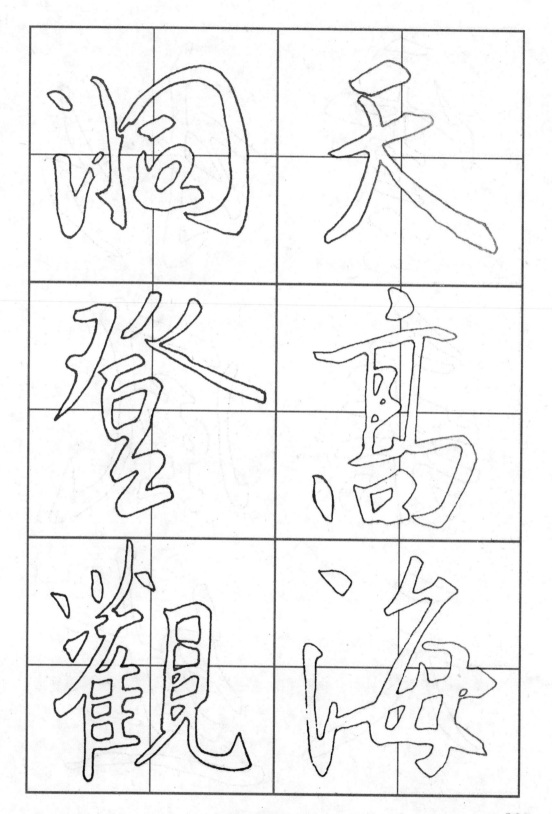

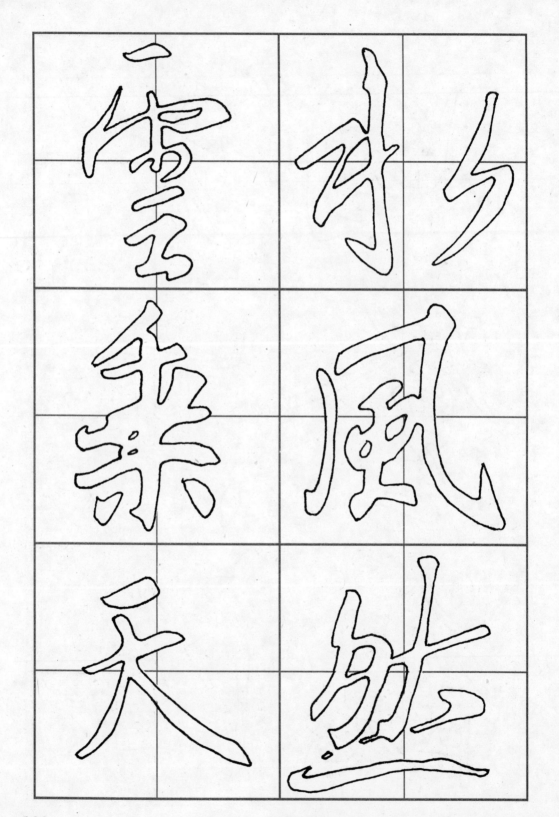

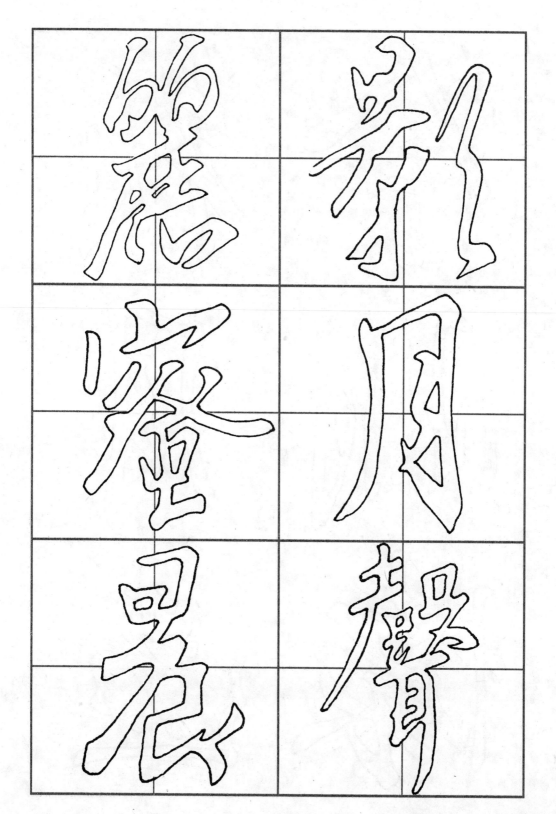

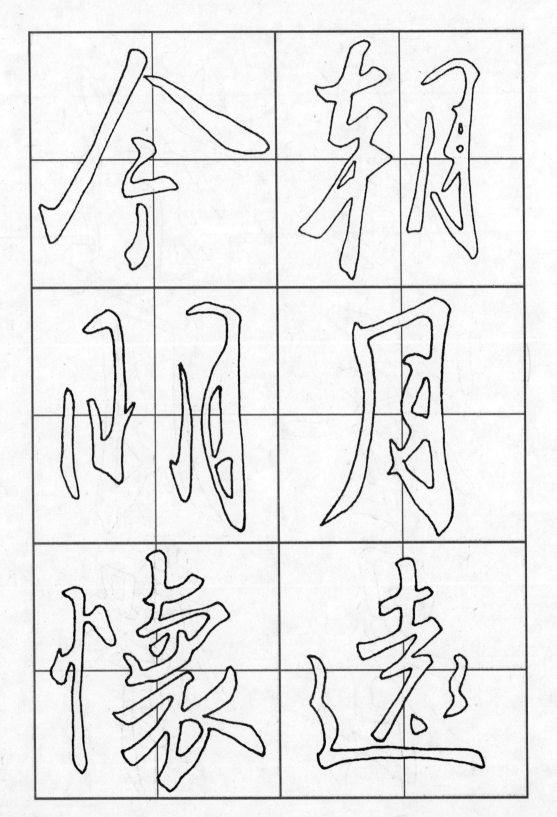

2. Diagonal-Marked Frame

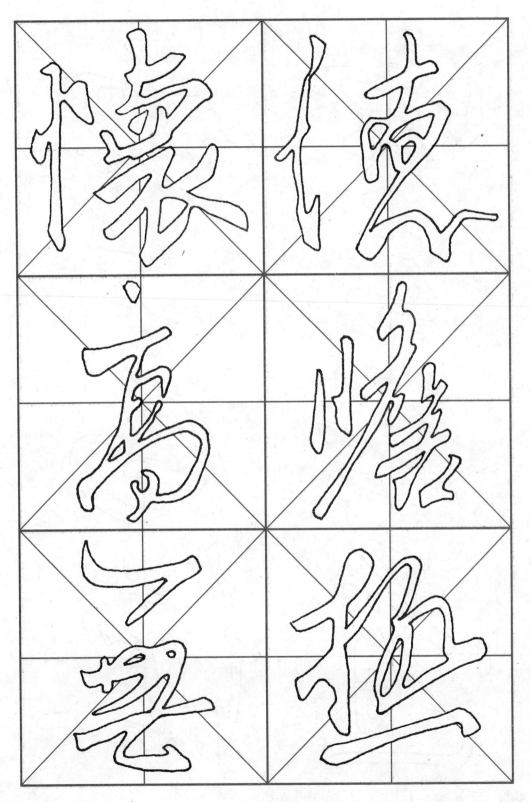

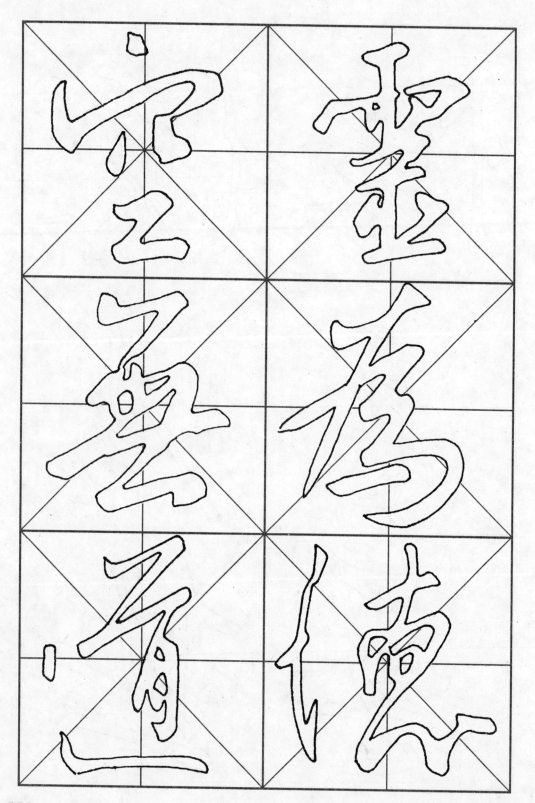

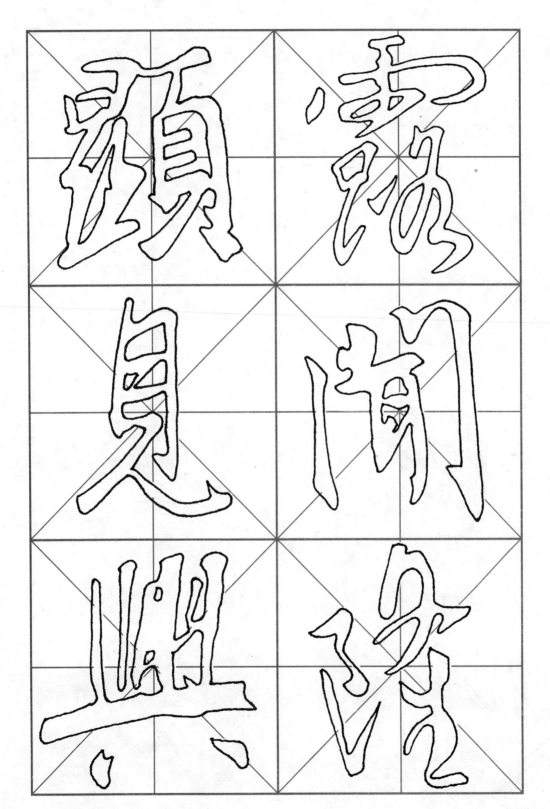

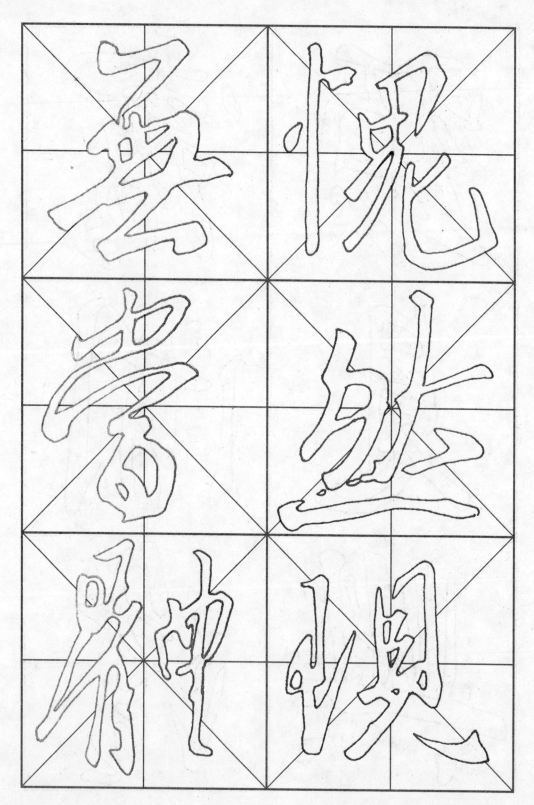

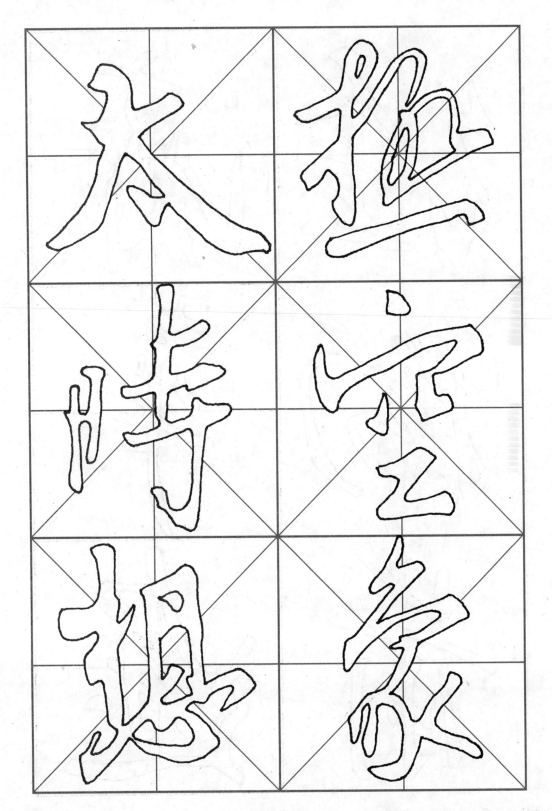

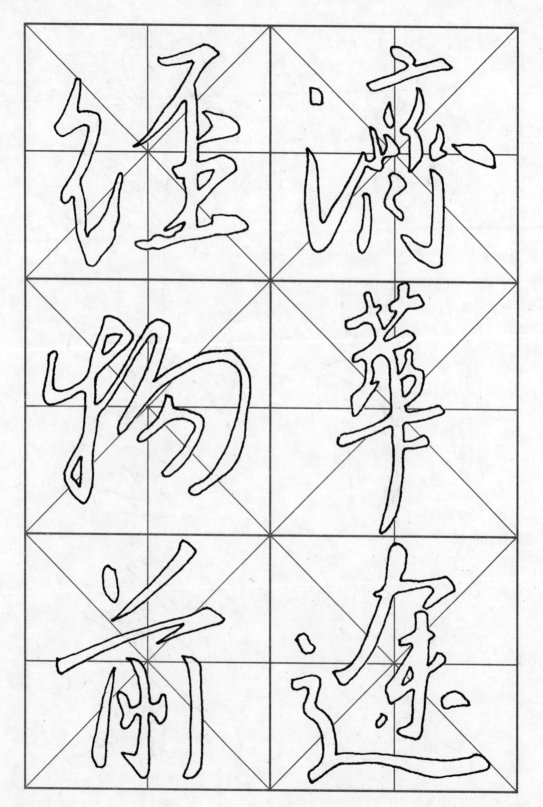

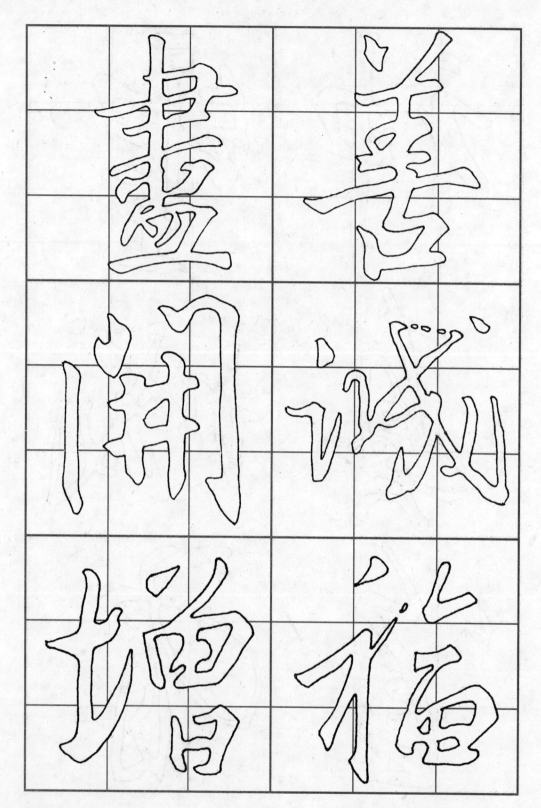

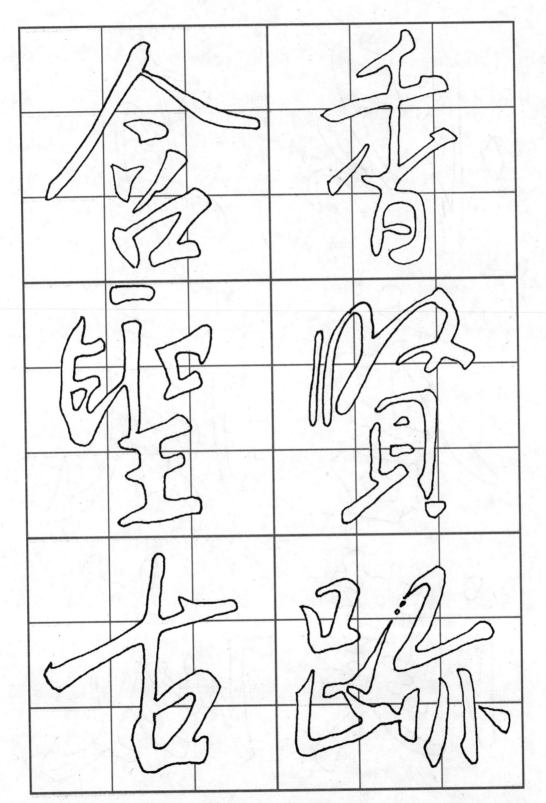

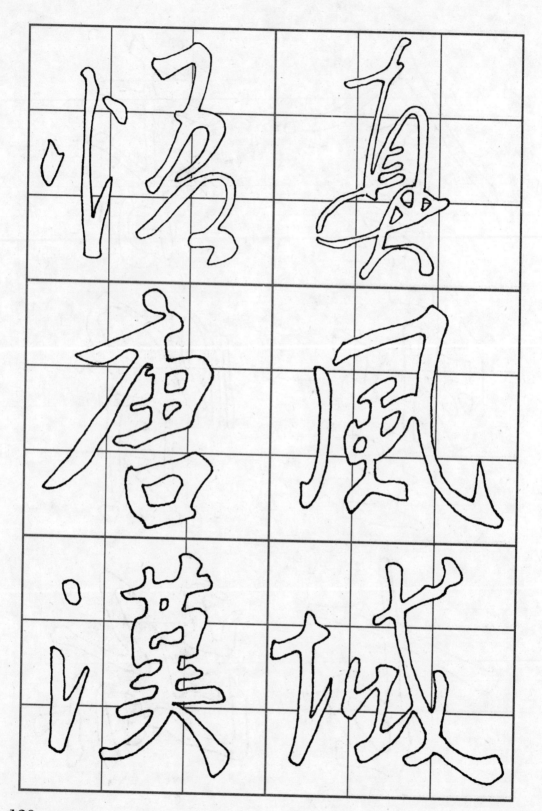

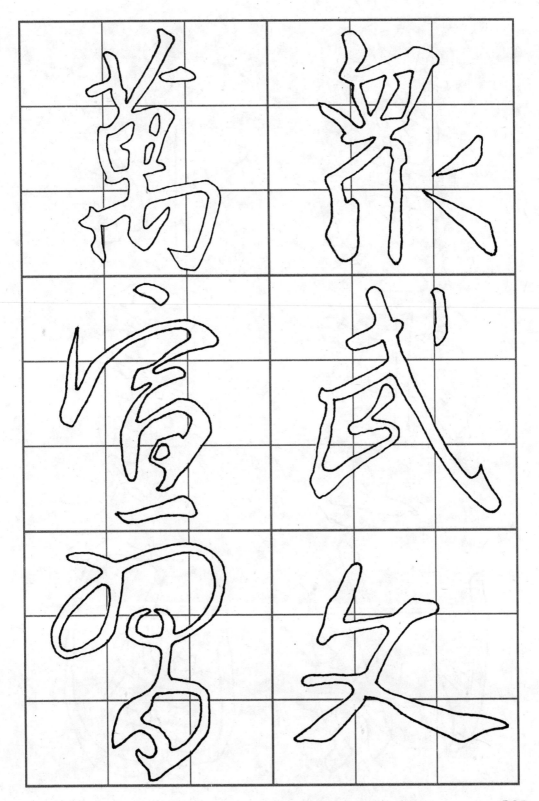

衆 萬
成 富
文 貴

4. Two-Square Frame

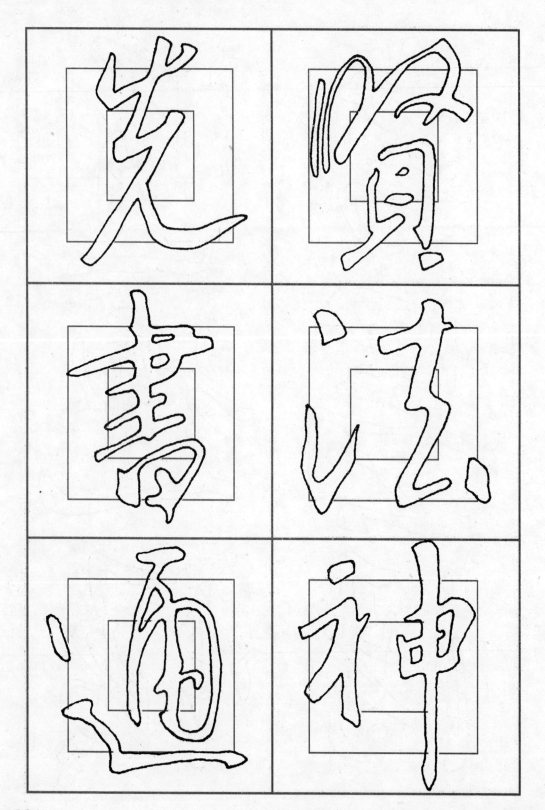

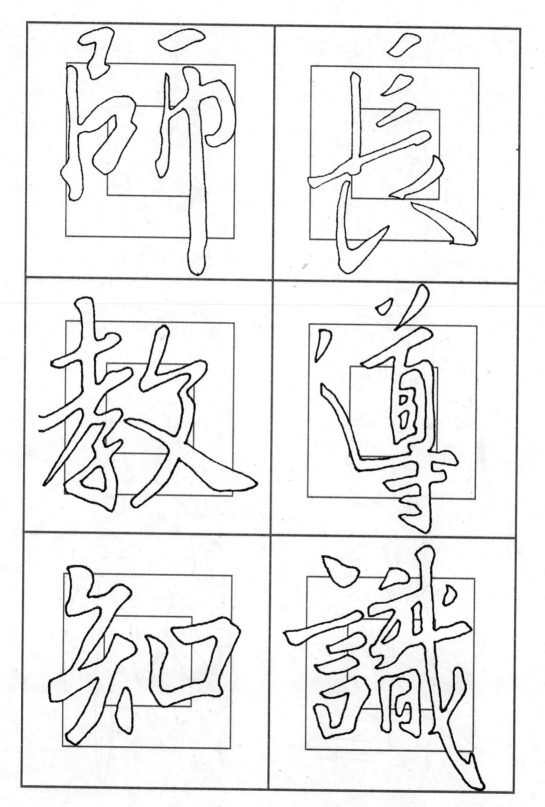

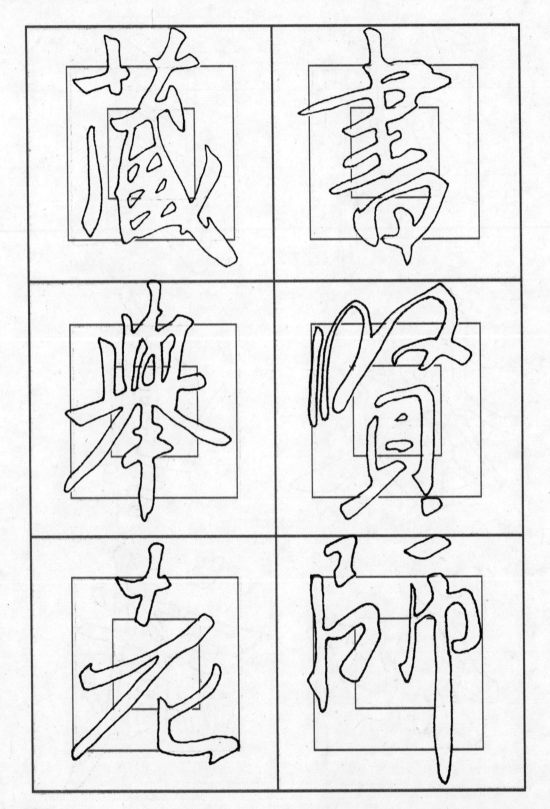

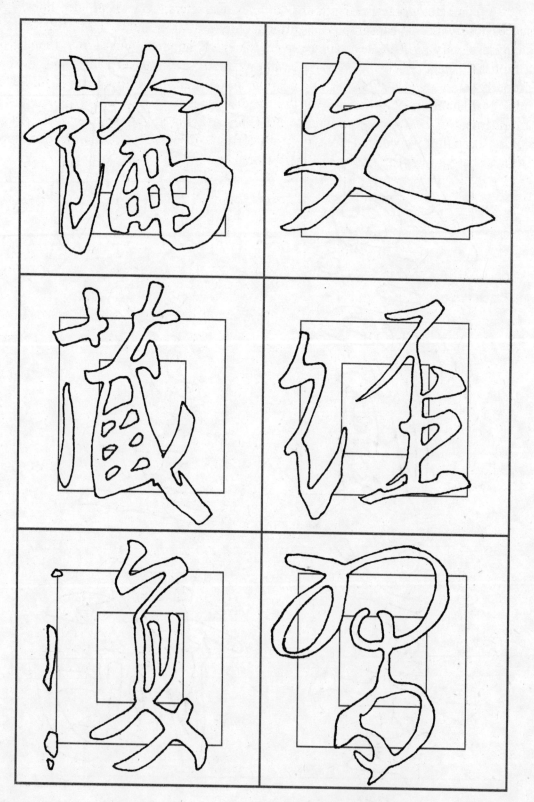

Chapter VII   The Art of Composition

"A character consists of strokes; a line, characters; and an article, lines." A successful work of calligraphy is often composed of a number of well-written characters, varying from several characters to several hundred, and even to more than a thousand ones. A character must be appropriately arranged in a line, and a line, properly set in a work. When writing a stroke or a character, a calligrapher should take into consideration the beauty of the whole piece of calligraphy. The artistic arrangement of characters and lines in the Chinese calligraphy is known as the art of composition, or was called "outlay," or "format" in ancient times. The charm of Chinese calligraphy can not be separated from beautiful outlay.

1. Various Forms of Scrolls

There are many forms of scrolls of Chinese calligraphy, mainly including central scrolls, antithetical couples, vertically hung, square, horizontal and hand scrolls, albums of calligraphy, round or folding fans, horizontal or vertical inscribed boards and a set of scrolls (mainly consisting of four, six, eight or twelve scrolls). A calligrapher adopts different forms of scrolls of Chinese calligraphy according to the actual needs and his/her appreciation. Different forms of scrolls are arranged in accordance with different arts of composition. A piece of well-written calligraphy and a well-arranged form of scroll may bring out the best in each other.

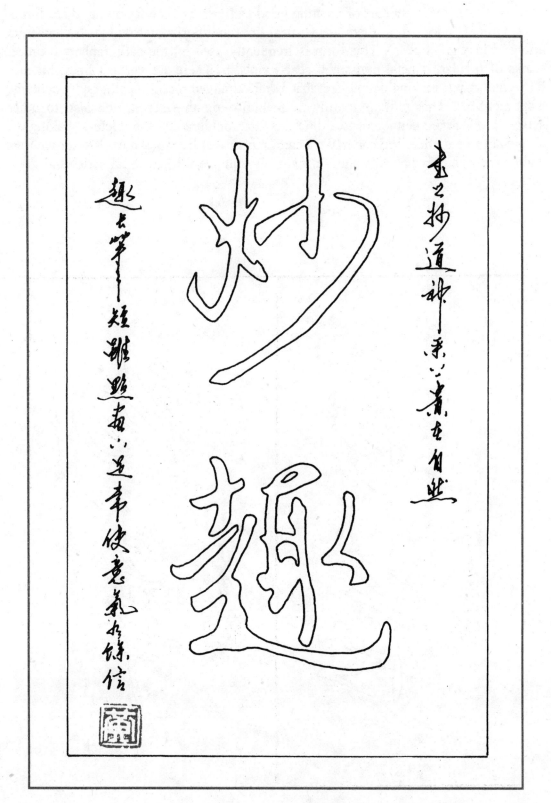

2. Text

The text is the main part of creating good calligraphy. The following three forms are commonly adopted: a. there are vertical lines and horizontal ranks, all characters arranged in a good order. This form is frequently used by the calligraphers creating works of regular, official and small seal scripts. b. There are vertical lines, but not horizontal ranks, making people feel that a well-arranged piece of calligraphy contains some changes. This form is mainly favorable to running script, and also to other scripts. c. There are neither vertical lines nor horizontal ranks. Completely shaking off all pre-set forms, this form can make a calligrapher feel free to express his/her feelings and create whatever he/she wants. It is mainly suitable for large seal script and grass script.

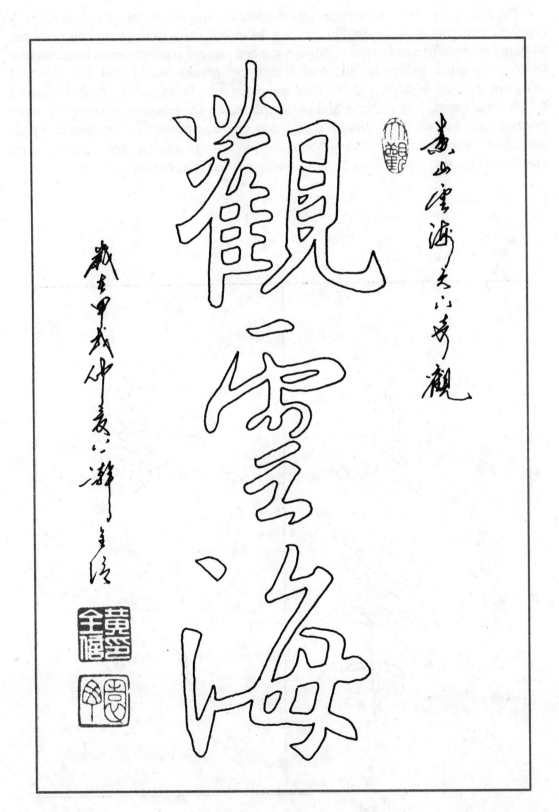

3. Inscriptions

The inscription is an indispensable component part of a work of calligraphy. A complete calligraphy work should at least have the calligrapher's signature at the bottom. Inscriptions can be classified into top and bottom inscriptions. The name of a recipient is often written at the top of the calligraphy work; and the name of calligrapher, at the bottom, with the date and place sometimes added. If there is only a bottom inscription, it is called a grass inscription. An inscription consisting of many words is called a rich inscription; and an inscription composed of a few words, a poor inscription. The inscription should adopt the same script as or a more cursive script than that of the text, rather than be more neatly written than the text.

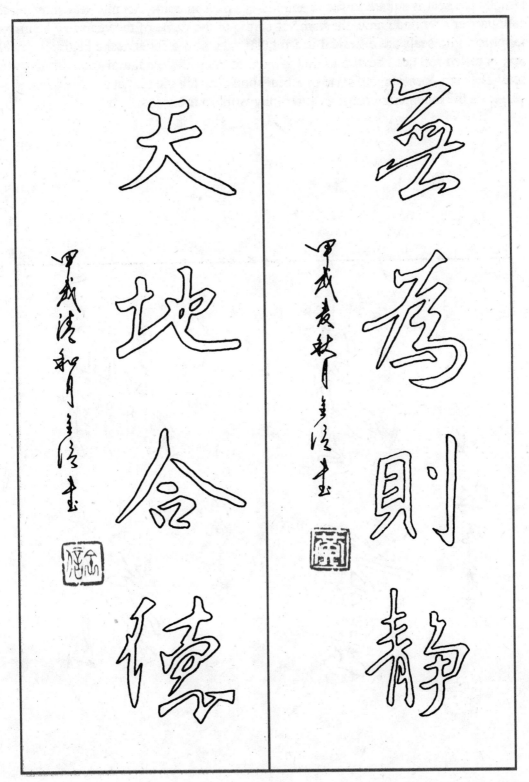

無為則靜

天地合德

4. Seals

In general, a seal should be affixed on a piece of calligraphy after the signature. Usually the seal is square in shape and red or white in color. An idle seal showing the calligrapher's refined name, the name of studio or the name of the year may be affixed too. Most idle seals are elliptical or irregular. The seal affixed at the beginning of the text is called the head seal; and that affixed at the middle edge of the text, the waist seal. The size, location and style of a seal should match the text and inscription. A red seal adds the touch that brings a calligraphy work to life.

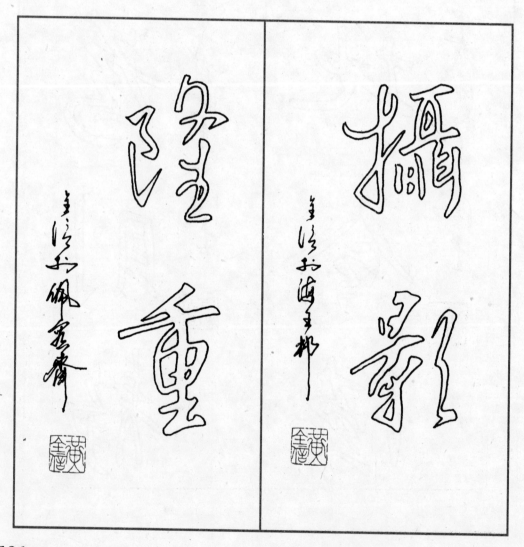

外師造化

中得心源

造化者自然墨也語出唐張彥遠歷代名畫記卷十載

唐張璪語甲戌暑日壬壬信擇許

Chapter VIII   Creation

The creation of a piece of calligraphy refers to the artistic labor for independently making a work of calligraphy. Before creating a piece of calligraphy, one is required to have obtained fairly high accomplishments and have a high degree of skill. While creating, one must pour all his/her feelings and thinking into his/her work to create a splendid space consisting of energetic dots and lines in long and short, curved and straight, square and round, slanting and straight, thick and thin, dry and moist forms so as to please both the eye and the mind.

1. Making a Plan Before Writing

Before one starts writing, one should make a well-thought plan concerning the text, inscription, seal, etc., prepare brush, ink and paper, decide how to write characters according to the size of a piece of paper, concentrate one's mind on the brush, spread out the paper prudently and start writing the first stroke resolutely. The profound significance of making a plan is to express the realm that the calligrapher has sought through a calligraphy work. This is hard with its abstract connotation. Without a plan, there would be no art. The Chinese calligraphers of the past ages paid great attention to making a plan, believing that the plan plays a leading role in creation.

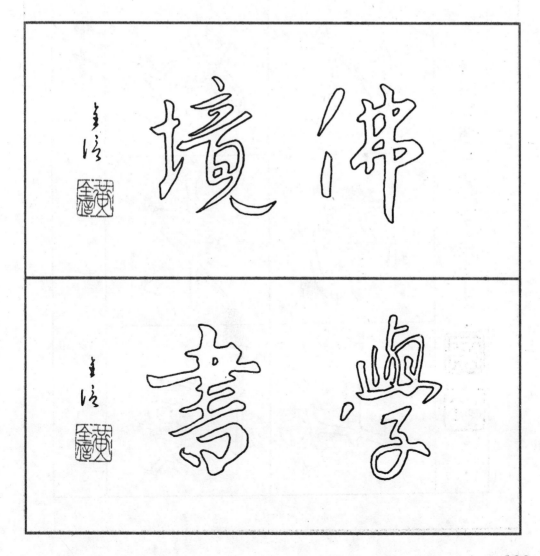

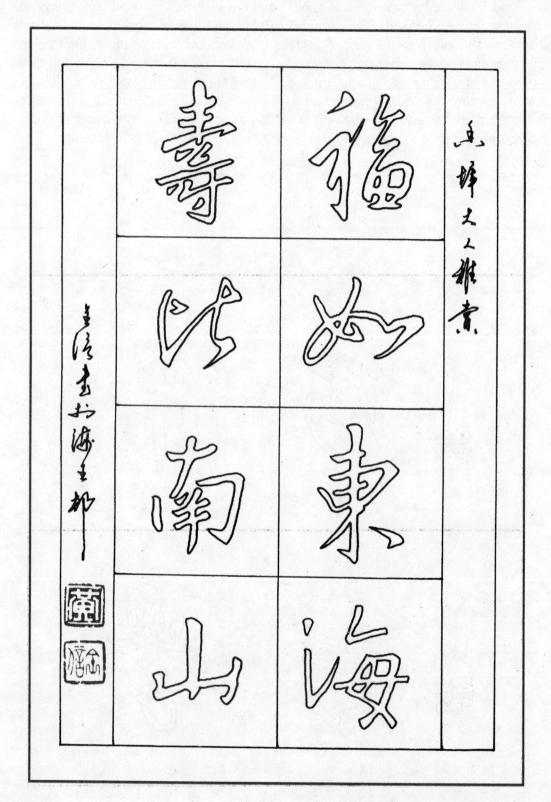

福如東海

壽比南山

玉坪文人雅書

重清書於海上都

2. The First Character Leads the Whole Text

"The first stroke sets the standards for a character, and the first character leads all characters of an article." This is brilliant elaboration in the *Calligraphy Manual* by Sun Guoting, a famous calligrapher of the Tang Dynasty, stressing the importance of the first stroke in the first character and the first character in a text.

The first character takes the lead of a calligraphy work, so it should be solid and striking rather than hollow and reserved. Writing the first stroke and first character well is just like a horse running ahead, followed by ten thousand galloping horses.

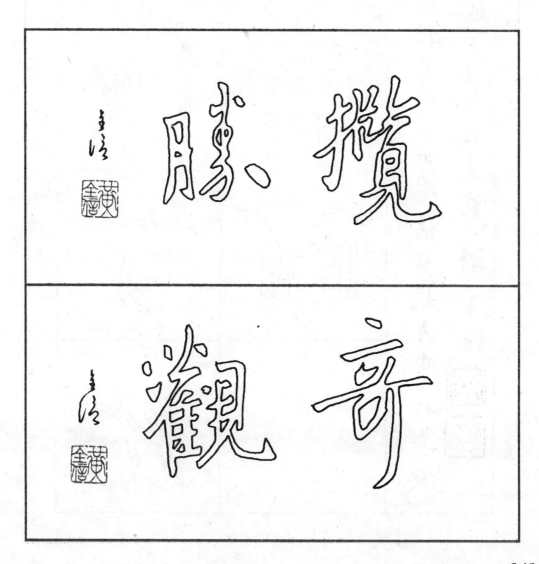

風儀与飲

月齋明月

南朝齊王儉褚淵碑文句風儀與秋月齊明音徽
與春雲等潤歲在甲戌至亥八浙生清

3. A Coherent Whole

Chinese calligraphy is particularly about coherence. Finishing a calligraphy work at one go aims at reflecting the unified internal spirit of a work. While creating a calligraphy work, one should try to finish it at one go, that means all strokes, characters, signature, etc. Coherence should exist throughout a piece of calligraphy, between characters and lines, which echo each other and are integrated into one, showing united spirit and charm.

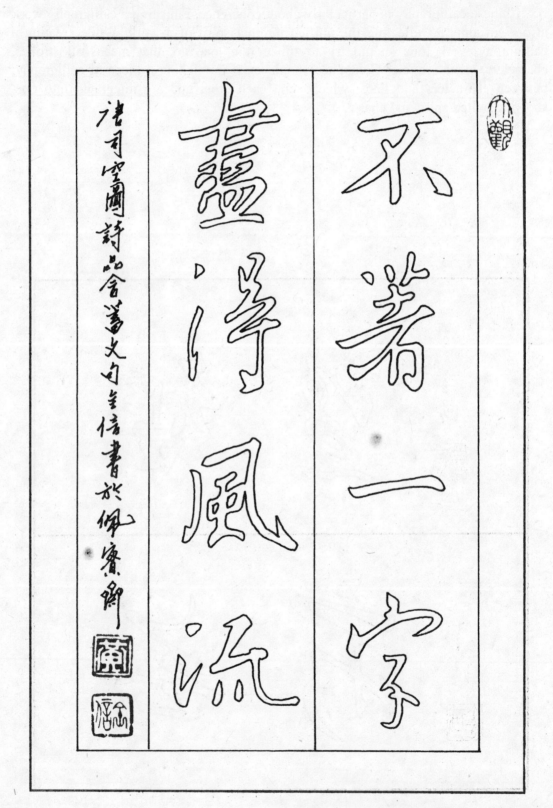

不著一字

盡得風流

4. A Poetic Conception

"A calligrapher expresses his feelings through his works." Before creation, a calligrapher should fully understand the meaning of a poem as well as its literacy grace, and should know well the author's original feelings. Only if one enters a poetic conception, can one fully and correctly express one's own feelings as well as the author's meaning. In addition, a calligrapher should pay attention to the unification of the script, style, contents, and so on.

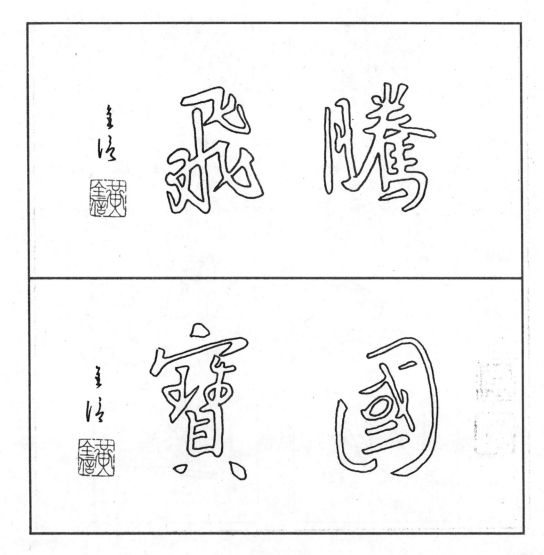

唐王维诗
明月松間照
清泉石上流

岁在甲戌春王洁玄佛象书

· 146 ·

Chapter IX   Appreciation

To improve the art of calligraphy, one should first copy one calligraphy model until one has a good command of it, and then copy various calligraphy models by different famous calligraphers; and then appreciate various calligraphy works of the past ages to constantly absorb nutrition and improve the appreciation level.

In addition, one is required to read a large number of books, make many trips, copy models of various schools and read a large number of tablets.

珣頓首頓首　伯遠勝

業情期群從之寶　自以羸患

志在優遊　始獲此出

意不剋申分別如昨　永為疇

古遠隔嶺嶠　不相瞻臨

晉王珣伯遠帖　甲戌春月金信

余每觀材士之作，竊有以得其用

心。其放言遣辭，良多變矣，妍

蚩好惡，可得而言。每自屬文，尤見

其精。恒患意不稱物，文不逮意，蓋

非知之難，能之難也。故作文賦

以述先士之盛藻，因論作文之利

乾隆丙子文徵書於清和龙別卅李

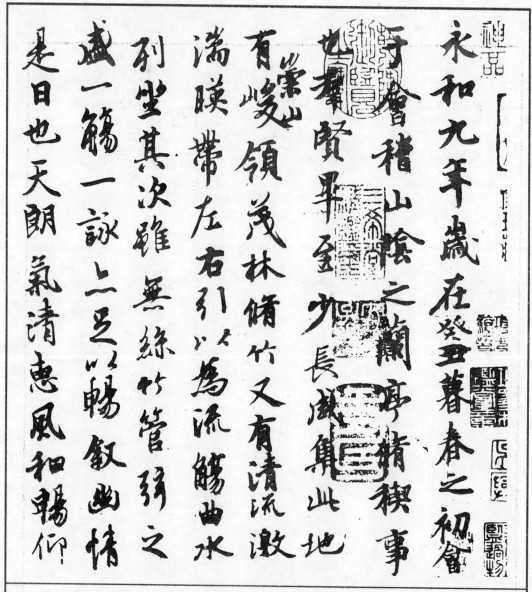

是日也天朗氣清惠風和暢仰
盛一觴一詠上足以暢敘幽情
列坐其次雖無絲竹管弦之
滿暎帶左右引以為流觴曲水
有峻領茂林脩竹又有清流激
崇山
列坐其次雖無絲竹管弦之
賢畢至少長咸集此地
也群
于會稽山陰之蘭亭脩稧事
永和九年歲在癸丑暮春之初會

On the third day of the third lunar month in the ninth year of the Yonghe reign period of the Eastern Jin Dynasty (317 – 420), Wang Xizhi got together with some 40 others at the Lanting Pavilion on Mount Shanyin. They drank wine and wrote poems to express their feelings. Wang Xizhi improvised a preface for the collection of the poems they had written – the *Lanting Pavilion Preface*. The calligraphy was praised by Mi Fu as the "the most exquisite running script under Heaven".

The *Lanting Pavilion Preface* consists of 28 lines, containing 327 characters in all. Among them there are more than 20 之, each in a different style. The preface fully demonstrates the super talent and skill of the "sage calligrapher".

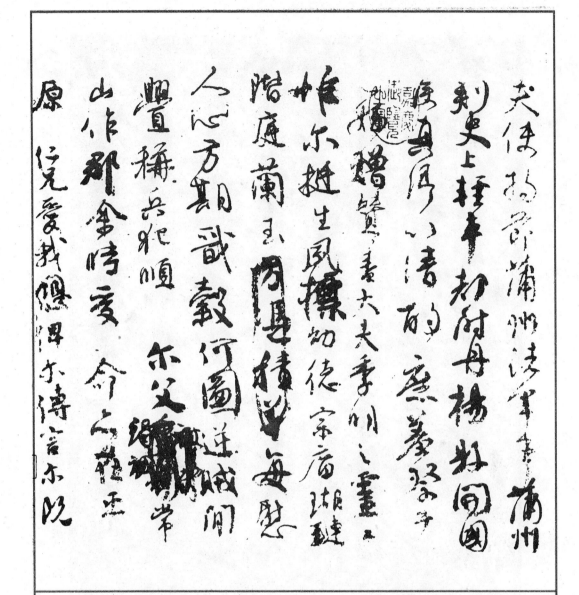

維乾元元年歲次戊戌九月庚午朔三日壬申第十三叔銀青光祿大夫使持節蒲州諸軍事蒲州刺史上輕車都尉丹楊縣開國侯真卿以清酌庶羞祭於亡姪贈贊善大夫季明之靈曰惟爾挺生夙標幼德宗廟瑚璉階庭蘭玉每慰人心方期戩穀何圖逆賊間釁稱兵犯順爾父竭誠常山作郡余時受命亦在平原仁兄愛我俾爾傳言爾既歸止

Funeral Oration to My Nephew was written by Yan Zhenqing at the age of 50. In the fortieth year of the Tianbao reign period of the Tang Dynasty Emperor Xuanzong, Yan Zhenqing and his brother Yan Gaoqing went on an expedition to suppress rebel forces led by An Lushan and Shi Siming, during which Gaoqing and his son were killed. Yan Zhenqing was so grieved that he wrote the oration at one go. The characters are broad and vigorous with a touch of tragedy. The piece is considered the "second-best example ever of running script".

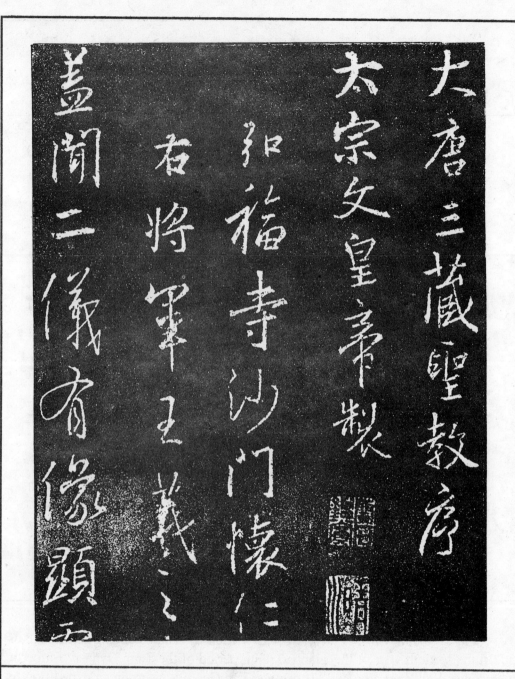

大唐三藏聖教序

太宗文皇帝製

弘福寺沙門懷仁

右將軍王羲之

蓋聞二儀有像顯

A monk in the Tang Dynasty (618 – 907) named Shi Huairen collected samples of Wang Xizhi's calligraphy in this article. He spent more than 20 years doing this. With its graceful style, rich variety of dots and strokes, and strict structure, the composition has long been considered the best textbook for learning running script.

责任编辑　单　瑛

封面设计　朱　丹　黄全信

图书在版编目（CIP）数据

行书自学教程 / 黄全信编著。－北京：华语教学出版社，1997.3
（中国书法自学丛书）ISBN 7-80052-456-6

Ⅰ. 行... Ⅱ. 黄... Ⅲ. 汉字－行书－书法－自学参考资料 Ⅳ. J292.11

中国版本图书馆 CIP 数据核字（97）第 00821 号

中国书法自学丛书—行书自学教程

黄全信　编著

*

©华语教学出版社

华语教学出版社出版

（中国北京百万庄路 24 号）

邮政编码 100037

春雷印刷厂印刷

中国国际图书贸易总公司发行

（中国北京车公庄西路 35 号）

北京邮政信箱第 399 号　邮政编码 100044

1998 年（16 开）第一版

（汉英）

ISBN 7-80052-456-6 / H · 548 （外）

03500

9 － CE － 3190P